Palgrave Studies in Cyberpsychology

Series Editor
Jens Binder, Nottingham Trent University, Nottingham, UK

Palgrave Studies in Cyberpsychology aims to foster and to chart the scope of research driven by a psychological understanding of the effects of the 'new technology' that is shaping our world after the digital revolution. The series takes an inclusive approach and considers all aspects of human behaviours and experiential states in relation to digital technologies, to the Internet, and to virtual environments. As such, Cyberpsychology reaches out to several neighbouring disciplines, from Human-Computer Interaction to Media and Communication Studies. A core question underpinning the series concerns the actual psychological novelty of new technology. To what extent do we need to expand conventional theories and models to account for cyberpsychological phenomena? At which points is the ubiquitous digitisation of our everyday lives shifting the focus of research questions and research needs? Where do we see implications for our psychological functioning that are likely to outlast shortlived fashions in technology use?

More information about this series at
https://link.springer.com/bookseries/14636

Tanya Machin · Charlotte Brownlow ·
Susan Abel · John Gilmour
Editors

Social Media and Technology Across the Lifespan

Editors
Tanya Machin
Faculty of Health, Engineering and Sciences
University of Southern Queensland
Toowoomba, QLD, Australia

Susan Abel
University of Southern Queensland
Toowoomba, QLD, Australia

Charlotte Brownlow
Graduate Research School
University of Southern Queensland
Toowoomba, QLD, Australia

John Gilmour
University of Southern Queensland
Toowoomba, QLD, Australia

Palgrave Studies in Cyberpsychology
ISBN 978-3-030-99048-0   ISBN 978-3-030-99049-7 (eBook)
https://doi.org/10.1007/978-3-030-99049-7

© The Editor(s) (if applicable) and The Author(s), under exclusive license to Springer Nature Switzerland AG 2022
This work is subject to copyright. All rights are solely and exclusively licensed by the Publisher, whether the whole or part of the material is concerned, specifically the rights of translation, reprinting, reuse of illustrations, recitation, broadcasting, reproduction on microfilms or in any other physical way, and transmission or information storage and retrieval, electronic adaptation, computer software, or by similar or dissimilar methodology now known or hereafter developed.
The use of general descriptive names, registered names, trademarks, service marks, etc. in this publication does not imply, even in the absence of a specific statement, that such names are exempt from the relevant protective laws and regulations and therefore free for general use.
The publisher, the authors and the editors are safe to assume that the advice and information in this book are believed to be true and accurate at the date of publication. Neither the publisher nor the authors or the editors give a warranty, expressed or implied, with respect to the material contained herein or for any errors or omissions that may have been made. The publisher remains neutral with regard to jurisdictional claims in published maps and institutional affiliations.

This Palgrave Macmillan imprint is published by the registered company Springer Nature Switzerland AG
The registered company address is: Gewerbestrasse 11, 6330 Cham, Switzerland

Foreword

Looking at the focus of much of the work on social media and technology use, you could be forgiven for thinking they are largely the domain of adolescents and emerging adults. The authors who have contributed to this book set about debunking that. As such, this book makes an important contribution to extending our understanding of how people at all ages engage with social media and use technology to support a diverse range of needs and purposes in developmentally relevant ways. As technology has become smarter and more mobile and has extended its reach down to the youngest and up to the oldest ages, it is increasingly important to understand the who, how, and why of use across the lifespan.

Laing and colleagues explore technology use at the earliest ages, birth to 6 years, which has been largely ignored in the extant research. While on the one hand, we have car seats and prams being equipped with tablet and other smart device holders designed for use by the children, we also have guidelines recommending no technology use under certain ages or strictly limiting time on technology that increases slowly with age. Yet, we still know very little about what these young children are using technology for and how different types and amounts of use affect their development and well-being. The research reported in this chapter suggests that it is the quality (type of content viewed, function, and context of use) rather than quantity (duration or frequency of use) that is important.

In their chapter on antisocial behaviour on social media, Branson and colleagues look at a topic that previously has almost exclusively focused on adolescents and emerging adults, probably because they were the earliest adopters of social media so have a longer history of use and, thus, period of research focus. However, social media use by adults has increased significantly in the last two decades so that there are almost as many users now in the 26–64 year-old age group as in the emerging adult age group (aged 18–26 years). Contrary to their expectations, Branson and her colleagues found that motives to use social media for cyberbullying and trolling was highest in 26–44 year-olds. This stage in the lifespan is an important time developmentally for commencing and consolidating careers and establishing relationships and parenting. Understanding how adult developmental challenges influence antisocial use of social media is important, yet currently under-researched.

Keeping on with the developmental theme, Stuart and her team address the question of how living out one's life on social media during adolescence affects identity formation by early adulthood and the important role that social connection to peers plays in that. Their results highlight that social media use is not straightforward in its effects on identity development. Greater online self-expression during adolescence both increased subsequent identity confusion but also enabled greater peer connection that decreased confusion and promoted identity consolidation.

What emerges across this book is that it is the how and why of social media and technology use that needs to be considered. Abel and Gilmour address this with respect to the role of the mobile phone in helping, and hindering, intergenerational connectedness and support-giving in kinship and community groups. Competing needs for privacy versus awareness of other's lives within groups in the digital era and the effects of getting this right on health are examined through a series of case studies.

The broader contribution that online social support makes to health outcomes is explored in more detail by Gilmour and colleagues. They examined how use of Facebook to connect with family and friends was related to physical and mental health and how that might differ between metropolitan and regional users. Interestingly, they found that Facebook-based social support was related to lower health concerns in metropolitan users, but there was no similar relationship for regional users. This result casts doubt on the commonly held idea that social media might be particularly beneficial for countering the tyranny of distance by enabling social support and, thereby, bolstering both physical and mental health.

However, technology does have a role to play in supporting health. Arguably, the biggest impact of technology on our health is via its ability to bring health services to us via telehealth. Accessing health services via online means reduces many of the barriers traditionally experienced by those who juggle work and caregiving. In their chapter, Russo and Werth explore the positive benefits of telehealth for achieving work-care balance.

Social media and technology have changed almost every aspect of how we live our lives, including how we grieve the end of the lives of those who are important to us. O'Connor and Kasket use longitudinal qualitative data to argue that, just as there is no one right or "normal" way to grieve offline, the same is true about the way people use social media to grieve the loss of loved ones. Social media provides another mechanism through which those who are grieving can tell their stories of the dead and their relationships with them and express their grief in their own unique ways.

Finally, it is worth noting that this book addresses not only the breadth of social media and technology engagement across the lifespan but does so using a broad range of methodological approaches. The methods encompass case studies, intensive daily diary recording, survey-based between-group approaches, and sophisticated longitudinal qualitative as well as quantitative methods. So, beyond the specific questions addressed and the new insights provided, this book also becomes a lesson in the diverse range of methodology relevant to answering questions about social media and technology use.

This book is perfect as a textbook for courses in social media and technology use from a developmental perspective that goes well beyond the typical reliance on adolescent and young adult use. However, it suits equally well as a reference for researchers who are studying social media and technology use and should stimulate further investigation.

Associate Professor Michelle Hood
School of Applied Psychology
Griffith University
Gold Coast, Australia

Contents

Introduction: Cyberpsychology Across the Lifespan   1
Tanya Machin, Charlotte Brownlow, Susan Abel,
and John Gilmour

**Technology Use of Children 0–6 Years of Age: A Diary
Study**   9
Kylie Laing, Tanya Machin, Michelle Adamson,
and Kristen Lovric

**Talkin' Bout My Generation: The Utility of Different Age
Cohorts to Predict Antisocial Behaviour on Social Media**   27
Molly Branson, Evita March, and Jessica Z. Marrington

**The Impact of Ease of Online Self-Expression During
Adolescence on Identity in Young Adulthood**   43
Jaimee Stuart, Riley Scott, Karlee O'Donnell, and Paul E. Jose

Communication, Social Support, and Families   61
Susan Abel and John Gilmour

**Links Between Telehealth, Work, and Caring
Responsibilities**   81
Fiona Russo and Shalene Werth

The Effects of Facebook-Based Social Support on Health Across Metropolitan and Regional Australians 97
John Gilmour, Carla Jeffries, Tanya Machin, and Charlotte Brownlow

What Grief isn't: Dead Grief Concepts and Their Digital-Age Revival 115
Mórna O'Connor and Elaine Kasket

Final Reflections 131
Charlotte Brownlow, Tanya Machin, Susan Abel, and John Gilmour

Index 135

Notes on Contributors

Susan Abel is an educator and researcher at the University of Southern Queensland. Her current research interests are family communication using social media, neurodiversity, and qualitative research methods.

Michelle Adamson is a registered psychologist of 20 years who has practised, lectured, researched, and supervised in the areas of child and adolescent psychopathology and family intervention.

Molly Branson is a current Ph.D. Candidate psychology at Federation University. Molly's research interests include cyberpsychology and online behaviour. In particular, Molly is interested in women's digital experiences, and how abusive behaviours such as cyberstalking, cyber dating abuse, gender-based online harassment, and image-based abuse manifest in online environments.

Charlotte Brownlow Associate Professor Charlotte Brownlow. Charlotte is the Associate Dean of the Graduate Research School at the University of Southern Queensland. Charlotte's research interests focus on diversity and difference, particularly in the area of neurodiversity. She is interested in the co-production of research with community members and has recently worked on a funded research project for Positive Partnerships, Australia. Charlotte leads the Neurodiversity research stream within the Health and Social Justice research theme in the Centre for Health Research at USQ.

John Gilmour completed a Doctor of Philosophy in 2020, which focused on the use of Facebook as a mechanism for social support, and it's effects on health outcomes. Dr. Gilmour is a Postdoctoral Research Fellow at the University of Queensland's School of Social Sciences, and a Lecturer at the University of Southern Queensland, with a research focus in social media, health, and crime, as well as the use statistics and research methodology in modern policing research.

Dr. Carla Jeffries is a psychological scientist and educator, and Undergraduate Psychology Program Director at the University of Southern Queensland. She researches into wellbeing and social connection in a technological world, as well as supervising a number of Honours students conducting research in this area.

Paul E. Jose a Professor of Psychology at Victoria University of Wellington, has studied social development in childhood and adolescence in many different settings for over 40 years, with a particular focus on peer relationships, identity, and social connectedness. As a researcher in developmental psychology, he has sought to examine development with longitudinal studies and has published papers and a book to encourage optimal examination of intra-individual change.

Dr. Elaine Kasket is a psychologist, writer, and keynote speaker. She is a Fellow of the Royal Society of Arts and an Associate Fellow of the British Psychological Society. Elaine has published numerous journal articles, book chapters, and books. Elaine's primary research interests sit at the intersection of psychology and digital-age technologies and she regularly speaks with the media about life, death, privacy rights, and the power of big tech while maintaining a busy psychotherapy practice for individuals and couples.

Kylie Laing originally completed a Bachelor of Business at James Cook University and worked in marketing and administration for the first part of her career. Feeling unfulfilled and wanting to help people and contribute to the community, Kylie realised a great interest in psychological science. She completed the Bachelor of Science (Psychology) degree in 2015 and went on to gain First Class Honours in 2018, studying both remotely through the University of Southern Queensland. During her honours thesis Kylie studied under the guidance of Dr. Tanya Machin and

Dr. Michelle Adamson conducting a diary study and researching technology use of young children. Currently focussing on her own young family Kylie hopes to continue her psychology journey in 2022.

Kristen Lovric Psychologist, Dr. Kristen Lovric is a casual academic staff member at the University of Southern Queensland, Australia. Kristen has experience in the delivery of psychological intervention services for individuals, families, and groups, and her research has involved investigation of psychological and social factors that influence human behaviour.

Dr. Tanya Machin is a psychological scientist and educator, and Associate Dean (Academic) of the Faculty of Health, Engineering, and Sciences at the University of Southern Queensland. She lectures and researches into the intersection of social media and technology with developmental psychology, as well as supervising a number of Ph.D. completing their research in this area.

Dr. Evita March is a leading national expert in cyberpsychology. Dr. March explores the psychology of online behaviour and has researched a variety of online behaviour including cyberbullying, trolling, cyberstalking, and online dating. In 2019, Evita presented a TEDx talk on empathy and cyber abuse, and in 2020 was selected as one of the ABC's Top Five early career researchers in science. Evita is a member of the International Society for the Study of Individual Differences (ISSID) and is the founder of ACORN (Australasia Cyberpsychology Online Research Network, est. 2020).

Dr. Jessica Z. Marrington is a Senior Lecturer in the School of Psychology and Counselling at the University of Southern Queensland. Dr. Marrington's research interests include fundamental cognitive processes, self-regulation, personality, and online behaviour. At present, her program of research is exploring Australian adolescent behaviours online, with a particular interest in the common occurrences of internet trolling.

Dr. Mórna O'Connor research it about grief in the digital age, when the dead can leave digital traces—of lives lived and relationships past—that can factor in grieving. Mórna is currently a postdoctoral researcher at the School of Health Sciences at the University of Nottingham in the United Kingdom.

Karlee O'Donnell is a current Ph.D. candidate in the School of Applied Psychology, Griffith University. Karlee is a passionate advocate for promoting the voices and needs of young people, with a particular interest in understanding factors that enhance or undermine thriving during adolescence and young adulthood. Her research to date has primarily focused on how experiences in online environments shape psychosocial well-being for those aged 13–25 years. For her Ph.D., Karlee is investigating how young adults' motivations for self-disclosure on social networking sites align with their developmental needs and the implications of these motivations on daily affect and social connection.

Dr. Fiona Russo is a Lecturer in HR, Management, and Leadership at USQ. Her principal area of interest is in the systemic response to varied and individual circumstances and the end of one-size-fits-all solutions in organisations across both public and private sectors. She has a particular interest in inclusive healthcare provision and works with Children's Health Queensland as co-Chair of both the Family Advisory Council and the Family Centred Care Committees. In this capacity, she contributes to the development of and improvements to patient-and family-centred health services for children and young people.

Riley Scott is a current Ph.D. candidate in the School of Applied Psychology at Griffith University. Her research interests focus on how adolescents and young adults perceive and use the internet and social media. Specifically, her Ph.D. research investigates how young adults develop and maintain close friendships across online and offline contexts, and how context-specific affordances and experiences unique to the digital environment affect how people think, feel, and act online. Riley is particularly interested in determining whether there are benefits of social internet use for the well-being of socially vulnerable youth.

Jaimee Stuart is a Senior Lecturer in the School of Applied Psychology at Griffith University. Her research focuses on positive development for young people with a focus on the interrelationships between cultural and cyber psychologies. Dr. Stuart is particularly interested in understanding patterns of risk and resilience on and offline for those who are minorities (ethnic, religious, gender and sexual orientation) as well as youth who experience inflated risk factors (e.g., exposure to violence, low socio-economic status, displacement). Her research on youth and technology examines cyberaggression and victimisation, parental internet supervision, online disinhibition, social media use, and self-presentation.

Dr. Shalene Werth is a Senior Lecturer at USQ. Her research, service and teaching are focused around diversity and inclusion in the workplace. Her interests lie specifically in the practice- based ideas, strategies, and policy development necessary for a genuinely inclusive workplace. Her research has covered gender, disability, and chronic illness in the workplace and also disability in the context of students in the tertiary education environment. She is the Deputy Chair of the Diversity and Inclusion Committee in the Faculty of Business, Education Law and Arts.

LIST OF FIGURES

Talkin' Bout My Generation: The Utility of Different Age Cohorts to Predict Antisocial Behaviour on Social Media

Fig. 1   Mean differences for age cohorts and antisocial use of social media. Error bars represent Standard Error   34

The Impact of Ease of Online Self-Expression During Adolescence on Identity in Young Adulthood

Fig. 1   Path model assessing the associations between ease of online self-expression, peer connectedness, and identity outcomes in adolescence and young adulthood (*Note* $*p < 0.05$; $**p < 0.001$, solid lines represent significant associations, and dashed lines non-significant associations. Model fit = $\chi^2 (10) = 37.80$, $p < 0.001$; CFI = 0.96; SRMR = 0.04; RMSEA = 0.05; 95%CI = 0.03, 0.06)   56

Communication, Social Support, and Families

Fig. 1   Bev's birthday message (*Source* Personal communication, Bev. Used with permission)   73

The Effects of Facebook-Based Social Support on Health Across Metropolitan and Regional Australians

Fig. 1   The effect of Facebook-based social support on physical and mental health concerns (*Note* *ns = non-significant, FBB = Facebook-based. For ease of interpretation control variables, error terms, and covariances are not shown)   106

Fig. 2   The effect of Facebook-based social support on physical and mental health concerns in the metropolitan sample (*Note* *ns = non-significant, FBB = Facebook-based. For ease of interpretation control variables, error terms, and covariances are not shown)   107

Fig. 3   The effect of Facebook-based social support on physical and mental health concerns in the regional sample (*Note* *ns = non-significant, FBB = Facebook-based. For ease of interpretation control variables, error terms, and covariances are not shown)   107

What Grief isn't: Dead Grief Concepts and Their Digital-Age Revival

Fig. 1   The three interlocking dead grief concepts, their digital-age revival, and critiques   125

LIST OF TABLES

Technology Use of Children 0–6 Years of Age: A Diary Study

Table 1   Code book for content analysis   22

The Impact of Ease of Online Self-Expression During Adolescence on Identity in Young Adulthood

Table 1   Descriptive statistics and correlations between indicators at adolescence and young adulthood   52

The Effects of Facebook-Based Social Support on Health Across Metropolitan and Regional Australians

Table 1   Demographic information of both the regional and metropolitan samples   102
Table 2   Correlations, means, and standard deviations of the variables in the structural equation model ($N = 367$)   105

Introduction: Cyberpsychology Across the Lifespan

Tanya Machin, Charlotte Brownlow, Susan Abel, and John Gilmour

Abstract This introductory chapter focuses on the rising influence and importance of social media both within academic research and everyday contexts. The chapter reflects on this intersection with individual lives, providing the context for the primary focus on the edited collection on the meanings and impacts of social media within individual developmental trajectories. The key themes underpinning the edited collection are introduced, outlining the authored chapters comprising these. The chapters span intersectionality with social media at all stages of development, and

T. Machin (✉) · C. Brownlow · S. Abel · J. Gilmour
Faculty of Health, Engineering and Sciences, University of Southern Queensland, Toowoomba, QLD, Australia
e-mail: tanya.machin@usq.edu.au

C. Brownlow
e-mail: charlotte.brownlow@usq.edu.au

S. Abel
e-mail: Susan.Abel@usq.edu.au

J. Gilmour
e-mail: John.Gilmour@usq.edu.au

© The Author(s), under exclusive license to Springer Nature Switzerland AG 2022
T. Machin et al. (eds.), *Social Media and Technology Across the Lifespan*, Palgrave Studies in Cyberpsychology,
https://doi.org/10.1007/978-3-030-99049-7_1

the presentation of the purpose of the collection as a whole and organisation of the text is presented. The seven chapters that comprise the edited collection seek to explore the diversity of engagement with online platforms throughout the lifespan and draw on specific examples in exploring this.

Keywords Social media · Technology · Developmental psychology

Individual engagement with social media and technology is on the rise. The use and expansion of social media sites has rapidly escalated since the public release of Facebook in 2006, with currently 2.85 billion people globally using the app each month (Statista, 2021; Wilson et al., 2012). In country statistics tell us that most people are active users of social media in Western countries, for example 89% in Australia (Kemp, 2020); 72% in the UK (Tankovska, 2021); and 90% in the US (Kemp, 2021). While statistics are more difficult to find to provide an accurate picture in developing countries, the impacts of technology broadly and social media specifically have been highlighted by researchers (e.g., Udanor et al., 2016). Accompanying this rise in use by people, we are also seeing an increase in research focusing on social media and technology. This is hardly surprising given that this type of research is relevant and interesting to both academics and the general community. Indeed, research focusing on social media frequently crosses between academia and is assimilated into general understandings of its impacts, with frequent anecdotal evidence cited to back up the research findings concerning its impact. The findings of the influence of social media and technology are therefore commonly reported not only in academic journals, but also in more mainstream media, including via social media channels themselves. Accordingly, more and more research has begun to examine the impacts of social media on a range of phenomena such as depression, anxiety, and psychological distress in adolescents (Keles et al., 2021), the role it may play in providing psychological and social support for people living outside of large cities (Gilmour et al., 2019), and its role in connecting families who may live geographically distant (Abel et al., 2021).

One area of psychology that has had a keen focus on the impacts and meanings of social media and technology is developmental psychology, with researchers considering the influence of technology throughout childhood, adolescence, and into adulthood and beyond. With developmental psychology examining the physical, cognitive, and social development of individuals across the lifespan (Arnett et al., 2019) it is hardly surprising then that researchers have turned their gaze to examining the impact these tools can have on development—both positive and negative. Indeed, this growing field of research which investigates how technology shapes human psychology has become known as cyberpsychology. Therefore, as editors we wanted this book to take some of the common issues that would typically be discussed or highlighted in a developmental psychology book, and present specific research addressing both those developmental concerns with a social media and/or technology focus, thus creating a book dedicated to cyberpsychology with a developmental flavour. Each chapter is a stand-alone work but contributes to a better understanding of development and cyberpsychology more broadly. The following overview will incorporate an outline of the book's structure and what the reader can expect to find.

Key Themes

Accessing social media and other online sites is a popular daily activity regardless of age. Undeniably having access to the internet has changed the way individuals interact with others for both work and play. For instance, individuals can now contact family and friends through videoconferencing apps such as Messenger rather than making phone calls or having face-to-face visits (Abel et al., 2021). Not only has social media changed the way we communicate, but the rapid advances in technology have also contributed to that change (Ancis, 2020). Consider for instance the home computer. In the 1980s the home computer was bulky, large, and expensive with limited graphics capability. This meant that few homes had access to or could afford a home computer. Compare that to today's technology found in tablets, laptops, or even a smartphone as well as the availability, accessibility, and affordability of these technologies. These technologies are also no longer restricted to the home environment, and thus the portability of these devices means individuals can be constantly connected to the world regardless of time or place so long as there is an internet connection! The 7 chapters that comprise this edited collection seek to explore the diversity of engaging online throughout the lifespan.

As well as diverse patterns of engagement with social media and technology, understandings of the nature of social media are varied and a definition to capture that diversity has been problematic (Carr & Hayes, 2015). For the purposes of this edited collection, we take a broad view of social media and suggest social media is internet-based, that users may interact with others (i.e., through online dating apps or YouTube clips) or may pursue interests on their own (i.e., scrolling through an Instagram feed) or use as a collaborative activity (i.e., playing an online game). Indeed, social media has evolved significantly since its first launch and in current times is certainly broader than just social networking.

The diverse development of social media has meant greater engagement by individuals throughout the lifespan. Indeed, there are some restrictions associated with many social networking sites and if our conceptualisation of social media began and ended with social networking we would neglect the varied ways that people can and do engage. For example, many social networking sites have a minimum age that children must be before joining the site such as Facebook who require a child to be 13 years old before they join these sites. However, pre-teens or children may access these sites either through mediation with the parent present or, perhaps more commonly, by the child mispresenting their age (Livingstone et al., 2017; Weeden et al., 2013). Rather, it is important to include the broader landscape of social media, which includes, for example, very young children who may be using apps that parents view as enhancing creativity or as educational (Marsh et al., 2020). With this information in mind, Chapter 2 has a specific focus on investigating the technology use of children aged between 0 and 6, a developmental period often cautioned with the perils of online engagement.

One of the risks of being online and using social media is the exposure of antisocial online behaviour. While the majority of online interactions are designed to build and support social interactions, there are many people who engage in more antisocial behaviours including cyberbullying, trolling, flaming, or online harassment with negative outcomes experienced by the victim (Cheng et al., 2015). Concerningly, around 1 in 5 Australians under 18 experience some sort of online exclusion, threats, or abuse, with a similar number of young people admitting to engaging in antisocial online behaviours (eSafety Commissioner, 2021). However, antisocial online behaviours are not just limited to those aged under 18 but is something adults also experience. Consider the case of Charlotte Dawson—an Australian television personality who repeatedly experienced online death threats including being told to *go hang herself* (Moses & Hornery, 2012) and eventually committed suicide (O'Brien & Ralston,

2014). Drawing on these broader debates, Chapter 3 explores the more negative aspects of online engagements and draws on a developmental framework to explore antisocial motives to the use of social media with individuals aged between 18 and 59 years old.

Social media also provides an ideal venue to engage in identity exploration. Identity is a key issue across the lifespan with a well-developed identity providing a strong sense of self, along with connections to others (Arnett et al., 2019). Identity is a particularly salient topic for adolescents with a stable sense of self, frequently considered to be one of the key tasks of adolescence. Indeed, adolescence has long been recognised as a time a teenager will try out different roles to explore their values and beliefs before committing to a stable identity (Erikson, 1968; Marcia, 1980). Identity and self-presentation on the internet more generally, is an important developmental topic. How a teen presents themselves online reveals aspects of who they are and who they want to be (Subrahmanyam & Šmahel, 2011). In Chapter 4, Stuart et al. use longitudinal data from New Zealand to investigate the concurrent associations between online self-expression, peer connectedness, and identity development in teens.

Social media is the ideal place for individuals to create and maintain their social connections. Indeed, social networking sites allow users to interact with multiple people in multiple social relationships all at the same time! Social networking sites also allow people with an alternate method of social connection for those who are unwilling or unable to contribute to social interactions in more traditional ways (Grieve et al., 2013). Social networking sites also can be a source of social support for others, with a recent systematic literature review demonstrating higher levels of Facebook-based social support predicting positive psychological and physical health outcomes (Gilmour et al., 2019). In Chapter 5, Abel and Gilmour explore how social media is not only a place for young people, but is also a place of support, entertainment, and conflict across the lifespan. They explicitly explore each developmental stage and discuss how individuals and families are utilising social media to connect and provide support.

During 2020, the world changed significantly with the novel coronavirus (COVID-19) pandemic. Globally, we saw social distancing measures including stay-at-home measures implemented to minimise the spread of the virus (Department of Health, 2020). Specific directives included the limiting of the numbers of people within certain sized spaces and many businesses were encouraged to have their employees work remotely. This meant technology was heavily relied upon both for social connection and remote-work arrangements (Mitchell, 2020). For businesses that previously relied on face-to-face arrangements—such as medical practitioners, the uptake of telehealth services was high. However, working from home has unique challenges for employees and specifically for those employees with children, who not only had to manage their daily work via technology but also their children's education when schools were also closed. In Chapter 6, Russo and Werth explore both the impacts of telehealth and the work-life balance for people who must manage both work and caregiving responsibilities.

Remote connection has frequently been a factor for the everyday lives of millions of people who live in rural and remote communities, often many miles from the nearest large city. Previously such communities relied heavily on technologies associated with the telephone, but in more recent times, online media has facilitated connection not just with others in the same country, but connection in a true global sense. Such differing layers of connectedness see online media being used to connect with geographically local and disparate community, provide a potential bridge for geographical barriers. One country that has experienced the challenges of remote living is Australia, and in Chapter 7, Gilmour, Jeffries, Machin, and Brownlow explore the social media use of geographically isolated Australians.

The culmination of developmental psychology books usually focuses on death, dying, and bereavement, and in some ways this book is no different. While life expectancy rates have increased over the last 25 years, we will all eventually die. When our families or friends do die, we are faced with the experience of grief—the emotional distress that accompanies the loss of our loved ones. However, given many of us have social media profiles within the different social networking sites we use, what happens with our digital footprint? We leave much more information now about ourselves than previous generations where all that was left was an elaborate headstone, and so it is pertinent to think about grief and the digital world. Chapter 8 does just that with O'Connor and Kasket using longitudinal qualitative data to problematise the digital-age reanimation of dead grief concepts and illustrate their continued inappropriateness for contemporary grievers.

The final chapter of this book, Chapter 9, seeks to examine the diverse use and engagement with technology and social media across the lifespan and reflect on the opportunities afforded by and the potential costs of engagement online. As such the content of these chapters is diverse but deliberately focused on topics relevant to developmental psychology and cyberpsychology. At the same time, chapter authors have used different types of methodologies beyond a purely quantitative approach to explore the nuances for individuals engaging with technology. Finally, this edited collection is unique in its focus on the collaboration with research students, to showcase not only recent work but provide a platform for students and recent graduates to showcase their work and collaboratively contribute to the emerging and ever-changing narrative surrounding technology and development.

REFERENCES

Abel, S., Machin, T., & Brownlow, C. (2021). Social media, rituals, and long-distance family relationship maintenance: A mixed-methods systematic review. *New Media & Society, 23*(3), 632–654.

Ancis, J. R. (2020). The age of cyberpsychology: An overview. *Technology, Mind, and Behavior, 1*(1).

Arnett J. J., Chapin, L., & Brownlow C. (2019). *Human development: A cultural approach* (Australian and New Zealand ed.). Pearson.

Carr, C. T., & Hayes, R. A. (2015). Social media: Defining, developing, and divining. *Atlantic Journal of Communication, 23*(1), 46–65. https://doi.org/10.1080/15456870.2015.972282

Cheng, J., Danescu-Niculescu-Mizil, C., & Leskovec, J. (2015, April). Antisocial behavior in online discussion communities. In *Ninth International AAAI Conference on Web and Social Media*. https://www.aaai.org/ocs/index.php/ICWSM/ICWSM15/paper/viewFile/10469/10489

Department of Health. (2020). *Physical distancing for coronavirus (COVID-19)*. https://www.health.gov.au/news/health-alerts/novel-coronavirus-2019-ncov-healthalert/how-to-protect-yourself-and-others-from-coronavirus-COVID-19/physicaldistancing-for-coronavirus-COVID-19

Erikson, E. H. (1968). *Identity: Youth and crisis*. Norton.

eSafety Commissioner. (2021, July 8). *Cyberbullying*. https://www.esafety.gov.au/key-issues/cyberbullying

Gilmour, J., Machin, T. M., Brownlow, C., & Jeffries, C. (2019). Facebook-based social support and health: A systematic review. *Psychology of Popular Media, 9*(3), 328. https://doi.org/10.1037/ppm0000246

Grieve, R., Indian, M., Witteveen, K., Tolan, G. A., & Marrington, J. (2013). Face-to-face or Facebook: Can social connectedness be derived online? *Computers in Human Behavior, 29*(3), 604–609. https://doi.org/10.1016/j.chb.2012.11.017

Keles, B., McCrae, N., & Grealish, A. (2021). A systematic review: The influence of social media on depression, anxiety, and psychological distress in adolescents. *International Journal of Adolescence and Youth, 25*(1), 79–93. https://doi.org/10.1080/02673843.2019.1590851

Kemp, S. (2020). *Digital 2020: Australia*. https://datareportal.com/reports/digital-2020-australia?rq=australia

Kemp, S. (2021). *Digital 2021: The United States of America*. https://datareportal.com/reports/digital-2021-united-states-of-america?rq=USA

Livingstone, S., Ólafsson, K., Helsper, E. J., Lupiáñez-Villanueva, F., Veltri, G. A., & Folkvord, F. (2017). Maximizing opportunities and minimizing risks for children online: The role of digital skills in emerging strategies of parental mediation. *Journal of Communication*, 67(1), 82–105. https://doi.org/10.1111/jcom.12277

Marcia, J. (1980). Identity in adolescence. In J. Adelson (Ed.), *Handbook of adolescent psychology* (pp. 159–187). New York.

Marsh, J., Lahmar, J., Plowman, L., Yamada-Rice, D., Bishop, J., & Scott, F. (2020). Under threes' play with tablets. *Journal of Early Childhood Research*, 1–15. https://doi.org/10.1177/1476718X20966688

Mitchell, V. (2020, March 20). *Report: Most Australian employees to work from home*. IDG Communications. https://www.cmo.com.au/article/672072/report-most-australianemployees-work-from-home/

Moses, A., & Hornery, A. (2012, August 31). Expert says Dawson broke the first rule of social media: Don't feed the trolls. *Sydney Morning Herald*. https://www.smh.com.au/technology/expert-says-dawson-broke-the-first-rule-of-social-media-dont-feed-the-trolls-20120831-254b6.html

O'Brien, N., & Ralston, N. (2014, February 22). Charlotte Dawson found dead. *Sydney Morning Herald*. https://www.smh.com.au/entertainment/celebrity/charlotte-dawson-found-dead-20140222-338j6.html

Statista (2021). Number of monthly active Facebook users worldwide as of 4th quarter 2021. Retrieved from https://www.statista.com/statistics/264810/number-of-monthly-active-facebook-userswordwide/#:~:text=With%20roughly%202.91%20billion%20monthly,years%20to%20reach%20this%20milestone

Subrahmanyam, K., & Šmahel, D. (2011). Constructing identity online: Identity exploration and self-presentation. In *Digital youth: Advancing responsible adolescent development*. Springer. https://doi.org/10.1007/978-1-4419-6278-2_4

Tankovska, H. (2021). *Social media usage in the United Kingdom (UK)—Statistics & facts*. https://www.statista.com/topics/3236/social-media-usage-in-the-uk/

Udanor, C., Aneke, S., & Ogechi Ogbuokiri, B. (2016). Determining social media impact on the politics of developing countries using social media analytics. *Program*, 50(4), 481–507. https://doi.org/10.1108/prog-02-2016-0011

Weeden, S., Cooke, B., & McVey, M. (2013). Underage children and social networking. *Journal of Research on Technology in Education*, 45(3), 249–262. https://doi.org/10.1080/15391523.2013.10782605

Wilson, R. E., Gosling, S. D., & Graham, L. T. (2012). A review of facebook research in the social sciences. *Perspectives on Psychological Science*, 7(3), 203–220. https://doi.org/10.1177/1745691612442904

Technology Use of Children 0–6 Years of Age: A Diary Study

Kylie Laing, Tanya Machin, Michelle Adamson, and Kristen Lovric

Abstract In this digital age, with access and use of technology constantly on the rise, young children now have more access to the internet and various technologies than ever before. Previous research suggests negative effects of technology use on child development, health and behaviour, which has led to recommendations to limit young children's technology use. However, little is known about technology use by young children. Thus, the aim of this research is to examine technology use in children 0–6 years of age. Eighty-one Australian parents completed a short questionnaire gathering information on household technology use; and fifteen parents subsequently completed a 7-day diary recording technology use by the child. A content analysis was used to analyse variables of interest including duration, frequency, context, devices used and content viewed, and function. Results indicated all households had access to the internet although the length of use for young children greatly varied. Children accessed technology throughout the day with content viewed primarily cartoons. This study highlights that for positive development

K. Laing · T. Machin (✉) · M. Adamson · K. Lovric
University of Southern Queensland, Toowoomba, QLD, Australia
e-mail: tanya.machin@usq.edu.au

© The Author(s), under exclusive license to Springer Nature Switzerland AG 2022
T. Machin et al. (eds.), *Social Media and Technology Across the Lifespan*, Palgrave Studies in Cyberpsychology,
https://doi.org/10.1007/978-3-030-99049-7_2

and well-being of young children, the content viewed, function, and context of technology use may be particularly important, not primarily the length of screen time. Further research into the elements such as the type of content viewed is required. Results may highlight the importance of interventions and updated guidelines aimed at assisting and supporting parents to achieve healthy early technology use.

Keywords Technology · Diary methods · Early childhood

Introduction

Access to and use of technology is on the rise with young children having more access to the internet and technology than ever before. For example, in 2017 an average of 7.8 devices were reported per family, with 99% of households using the internet via smartphones and 97% of children under 15 having internet access (Australian Bureau of Statistics [ABS], 2018). Young children's technology use has also become more commonplace with 79% of children aged 5-to-8 years regularly accessing online material in their homes (ABS, 2012), and 50% of toddlers and preschool-aged children using a screen-based device without any supervision (The Royal Children's Hospital [RCH], 2017). With technology and internet access more popular than ever, it is not uncommon to see young children 'glued' to a screen on a portable device at shops or restaurants (Holloway et al., 2013).

Technology can be a broad term. For this chapter we are defining technology as an electronic device including web or non-web applications (i.e., apps) used through a television (TV), DVD player, computers including tablets, smartphones, gaming consoles, hand-held games, and interactive watches. The term 'screen time' will be used to describe activities completed in front of an electronic/digital screen such as a child watching tv or playing a game. Currently, most of the research focusing on the impacts of technology and/or screen time concentrates on adolescents with a lack of literature on the effects in very young children—particularly those aged under 6-years old. However, as more research emerges it is clear there are both benefits and challenges to technology use.

Technology use and screen time can negatively impact development, health, and behaviour in children. Specifically, technology use may inhibit children's language development (Madigan et al., 2020), physical activity levels (Chonchaiya & Pruksananonda, 2008; Ferguson & Donnellan, 2014; Lagercrantz, 2016; Plowman et al., 2010) sleep quality, and self-regulation (Brown & Smolenaers, 2018; Cliff et al., 2018; Holloway et al., 2010; Kabali et al., 2015). Screen time has the potential to reduce outdoor play and increase sedentary behaviour, decrease face-to-face personal interactions with others as well as activities such as reading, with all these activities being conducive to healthy childhood development (Canadian Paediatric Society, 2017). Independent use of technology by a child can also lead to negative experiences such as access to inappropriate content (Barr et al., 2010; Holloway et al., 2010). Given these many concerns, governments have released recommended guidelines for parents. For example, the Australian Government (Department of Health and Aging [DoHA], 2018) released national guidelines advising that children under 2 should not be exposed to any screen time and 2–5-year-olds should be limited to less than 1 hour per day. These guidelines are similar to recommendations found in Canada and the United States (AAP, 2016; Canadian Paediatric Society, 2019). However, it should be noted the AAP (2016) does encourage activities such as video chats with relatives and co-viewing or well-designed programs such as Sesame Street viewed with an adult. More recently, the World Health Organisation (WHO, 2019) reinforced government guidelines, stating less screen time is a better option for very young children.

However, despite clear and universal recommendations, it is evident young children are still engaging with technology at an increasing rate. Specifically, it has been suggested young children watch screens in excess of existing guidelines (RCH, 2017). Results of a Australian Child Health Poll confirmed a third of parents did not place any restrictions on screen time or content for children aged less than 6-years old (RCH, 2017). It was reported 63% of children under 2 years of age were using screen-based devices, with an average of 14.2 hours of screen time per week, and 72% of 2- to 5-year-olds were using screen-based devices, with an average of 25.9 hours of screen time per week (RCH, 2017). Screen time thus appears to be in excess of the guidelines, even at young ages, and unfortunately, time spent on screens does increase with age (Holloway et al., 2013).

Early technology use can be influenced by many factors including the use of technology by parents and siblings (Holloway et al., 2010; Lauricella et al., 2015). For example, parents may use technology as a management strategy to engage children while parents' complete tasks (i.e., making dinner), as a sleep aid, a calming device, or as a reward (Brown & Smolenaers, 2018; Holloway et al., 2010; Kabali et al., 2015). Parents may also want their child to have access to the latest technology or apps for educational advantage (Plowman et al., 2010). Additionally, young children who have older siblings in the home may also be influenced and encouraged by their siblings to engage with screens, and are reported to commence using the internet earlier than peers without older siblings (Holloway et al., 2013).

The Current Study

Despite current recommendations regarding children's use of technology and minimising screen time, preliminary data on the use of technology by young children suggests these recommendations are not being followed by parents. However, there is limited data available on *how* young children aged under 6-years old are using technology. Several older studies have used diaries to gather data on children's technology use though these were limited by using brief 24-hour diaries (Barr et al., 2010; Ferguson & Donnellan, 2014; Zimmerman & Christakis, 2007). Diaries are an appropriate method of data collection as they provide advantages in gaining an accurate account of children's screen time activities over other self-reported methods (Määttä et al., 2017). Further, diaries can help mitigate the risk of bias by gathering data immediately after the time point of interest rather than relying on accurate recollection of an event.

Therefore, the overall aim of this study was to determine *how* young children (i.e., children aged under 6-years old) are using technology in their daily lives using a diary method. More specifically, our variables of interest included: (1) duration, frequency, and context (where and when) of screen time; (2) devices used and content viewed; and (3) function of technology use.

Method

Participants

Australian parents ($N = 81$) of children aged 0–6 years were recruited through online platforms (i.e., researchers' personal Facebook account), the host university, and personal networks to firstly complete an online questionnaire. Inclusion criteria for both the online questionnaire and the subsequent diary, required participants to be a parent or carer of a child who currently lives in their care and is aged between 0- to 6-years and uses technology. The online participants ranged in age between 19 and 52 years old ($M = 34.44$; $SD = 5.70$) with the target children aged five months to 6 years 8 months ($M = 3.61$ years, $SD = 1.84$). The participants were predominantly mothers (96.20%) who had completed some form of post-secondary education (84.48%).

After completion of the online questionnaire, eligible participants were then invited to participate in the diary study, with 55 potential participants requesting to take part in the research. The final diary sample comprised of 15 participants (27.3% participation rate) who completed and returned the diary. Diary participants were predominantly mothers (93.30%) aged between 31 and 44 years ($M = 37.93$; $SD = 4.28$), who had completed post-secondary education, mostly university studies (80%), followed by an advanced diploma or diploma (13.30%), and trade or apprenticeship (6.70%). The target child had a mean age of 4.19 years ($SD = 1.48$), with a range of 1 year 7 months to 6 years 3 months.

Instruments

Questionnaire. A 23-item online questionnaire was used to gather data on demographic variables and household technology availability and use (e.g., parents' own use of technology). For example, 'What technology do you have available in your household?' with a selection of different technologies including TV, smart TV, smartphone, tablet, computer/laptop, gaming console, hand-held game console, or other technologies. Once the questionnaire was completed, participants then indicated if they were willing to participate in the diary study.

Diary. The 7-day diary was designed to capture details about the target child's technology use while in their home environment. Parents recorded each instance of technology use over a typical week using a printable diary template. Questions were asked about the types of devices children used, what the child viewed, the length of use, who initiated technology use, reason for technology use, location of use, and what was happening directly before/after use. Parents were encouraged to report technology use while the child was in alternative care were possible (e.g., using a computer at day-care) in addition to non-use periods, and invited to provide further comments regarding children's use of technology.

Procedure

Ethics approval was obtained from the host university before any data collection took place. Parents interested in the study followed a link from online advertisements through to information about the study, an online consent form, and the online questionnaire. To identify a 'target child' to be the focus of the questions, parents were asked to list all children in their care, and a computer algorithm then randomly selected one child in the 0- to 6-year range. This child was then displayed on the screen to the parent with instructions asking the parent to only answer questions related to this specific child. After completing the questionnaire, eligible participants were then invited to take part in the diary stage by supplying their email address. That is, eligible participants had to have a child aged between 0-to 6-years who used technology. Parents were then emailed a paper-and-pen diary template including instructions on how to complete the diary. Participants were then asked to choose a 'typical' week and complete the diary daily over seven consecutive days. Completed diaries were returned via email and matched with questionnaire data via the email address. Participants were then assigned a pseudonym to ensure confidentiality.

Analyses

Quantitative data from the online questionnaire and diary was analysed using descriptive statistics such as frequencies, correlations, and t-tests using SPSS. The qualitative data comprised of the parents' comments and feedback and was analysed using content analysis (Krippendorff, 2004). Content analysis is a suitable research technique for diary studies through the interpretation of data in a replicable and valid system of coding (Krippendorff, 2004). Intercoder agreement helps to determine the reliability and consistency of the developed coding system and in the current study, two coders were involved, reading the entirety of the diary data (i.e., 148 technology sessions) before separately coding 21% of the total data. Coders then came together with any discrepancies resolved through discussion which resulted in high (>90%) inter-coder agreement (Lombard et al., 2002). In this research, a code book was then developed and assigned to interpret the information obtained within the context of the diary entries (Decuir-Gunby et al., 2011).

Replicability was thus enhanced through clear outlining of the coding system employed in the analysis. Coding was developed for data gathered under three distinct section of the diary: why was this technology used; what was happening before or when the child accessed technology; and what happened after the technology was ceased. Ongoing consistency was thereafter managed using a code book developed for each category. The resulting code book that was developed for each of the three categories is outlined in Appendix A.

FINDINGS AND DISCUSSION

Data on the availability and use of technology was captured through the questionnaire with parent usage reported as an average of 24 hours per week of home technology use ($M = 24.13$, $SD = 13.23$) including 8 hours use in view of the target child ($M = 8.47$, $SD = 6.27$). Smartphones and tablets were most prevalent followed by smart TVs, computer/laptops, with 93% of households accessing TV or mobile smart devices.

CHILD TECHNOLOGY USE

Duration, Frequency, and Context of Technology Use

The first variables examined the duration, frequency, and context of screen time and technology use. Over the week of the diary, the total time each individual child used technology ranged from 20 minutes to 22.5 hours ($M = 8.25$ hours, $SD = 5.99$). In comparison to Australian recommendations for children aged 0-to 2-years to have no screen time, the two children aged under 2 in this study were reported to use technology although this time varied widely from 32 to 103 minutes per day. This is a significant level of screen time, however less time than children aged under 2-years old in the RCH (2017) study which reported 14.2 hours per week. Similarly, government recommendations limit 2- to 5-year-olds to less than 1 hour of screen time per day, whereas participants reported an average of 70 minutes to use per day. Again, there was great variance with one child engaging in short 20 minutes sessions over the week to another who averaged 3.21 hours per day. Recommendations for children aged over 5-years old are restricted to a maximum of 2 hours per day, and in our study the children adhered to that recommendation, averaging 73 minutes. A one-way analysis of variance (ANOVA) was performed to establish the effects of age (0–2 years, 2–5 years, and 5 years and over) on the children's level of technology use. There was no significant effect of age group on length of technology use for the three conditions, $F(2,12) = 0.012$, $p = 0.988$.

The average number of technology use session per day for all children was between 1 to 2 ($M = 1.41$) and number of sessions per week ranged from one to 19 sessions ($M = 9.87$). The average length of session per child ranged from 20 minutes to 1.5 hours ($M = 47$ minutes, $SD = 21.36$). While children did use technology throughout the day, a noted peak in use was between 5–6 p.m. (25 instances), followed closely by 3–4 p.m. (15 instances) and 7–8 a.m. (12 instances).

With regards to context, and more specifically location, the children used the technology in open spaces within the home, in view of a supervising parent, ideally giving the parent a good idea of content being viewed by the child. Supervision of child technology use is highlighted by the AAP (2016) as an important factor in young children's online safety. More specifically, children used technology in an open area (i.e., a lounge or dining room; 74%). Other common locations were public spaces with parents (e.g., restaurant), at a friend or family members home, or a parents' workplace. However, this study did not assess direct parent supervision or interaction with the child's technology experience. As internet safety is a concern for young children's technology use due to the potential of negative experiences (Holloway et al., 2013) and risks of viewing adult-directed programs (Barr et al., 2010), further studies should investigate parental involvement in technology sessions.

Devices Used and Content Viewed

The second set of variables of interest examined what devices and content were being used and viewed by 0- to 6-year-olds. Having many devices as well as the internet available at home may make it difficult for parents to place restrictions on screen time or content viewed. Each household reported having at least three different types of devices available with an average of at least five different types of devices in the home. Devices included televisions (76%), tablets (10%), smartphones (8%), laptops and computers (5%), and gaming consoles (1%).

Both children under 2-years old only viewed a TV, with most of the children over 4-years old reported to have regularly viewed content on a smartphone or tablet, again consistent with RCH (2017) findings. Content viewed by the children included ABC Kids and TV or movies as the most viewed content (36 and 21% respectively), Netflix (15%), and YouTube (12%). Gaming apps and consoles were the next most popular content at 6 and 3% respectively. The remainder of the content included educational websites and apps, with this totalling 4%. General TV viewing was often reported as cartoons (66%), and family movies (28%). These results are also consistent with Holloway et al. (2013) who reported entertainment as the main content watched.

Content viewed on devices has been noted to have differing impacts on a child's development, with greater negative outcomes associated with watching non-educational programs (Holloway et al., 2013; Johnson & Puplampu, 2008). Alternatively, educational programs and apps may offer benefits for learning such as creative play, positive racial attitudes, and language development (Holloway et al., 2013; Wartella et al., 2010); all while not impeding executive functioning compared to other content (Huber et al., 2018). However, it should be noted that parents in this study often did not specify program names instead they broadly listed content as ABC Kids, YouTube, or Netflix. It may be that some of the programs viewed were educational in nature but were unable to be categorised as such during coding. Future research would benefit from gathering specific program-relevant information.

The Function of Technology Use

The variables of interest focused on the function of technology use. Findings showed the primary reason for the child engaging with technology was for entertainment purposes (63%), followed by a strategy for parents to complete activities uninterrupted so they could engage in activities such as preparing a meal or showering, completing paid work, grocery shopping, or quiet time (25%), and then as part of a bedtime routine (5%). Approximately half of the technology sessions reported (49%) were parent-initiated. These findings also provide support for previous studies (Brown & Smolenaers, 2018; Holloway et al., 2014; Kabali et al., 2015), however, contrary to prior findings, parents in the current study did not report using technology to calm their child in public when they were misbehaving or as a reward (Brown & Smolenaers, 2018; Holloway et al., 2014; Kabali et al., 2015). Interestingly some of the reasons for using technology were as part of the child's bedtime routines and daily routines (i.e., getting ready for the day), which raises the question of whether parents are using technology as a tool of distraction to get their children ready to complete a task. And just as educational programs were not common content for viewing, educational motives for use of technology also did not feature highly.

We also included questions in the diary focusing on both what circumstances were occurring before and after technology use, to examine whether there were any emotional and/or behavioural antecedents or consequences. Prior to technology use children were generally involved in normal daily routines (31%), home play (31%), and sleeping (16%). Most technology sessions that occurred after sleeping were often initiated first thing in the morning upon the child waking, often as early as 5.30 a.m. In 3% of sessions, emotional instances (such as temper tantrums) did precede technology use, with parents using technology to settle the child in their own home.

Activities parents reported after technology sessions concluded included normal daily routines such as bathing (44%), home play (22%), unclassified activities (15%), and sleeping (4%). Approximately one in ten sessions of technology use were reportedly followed by emotional demands for continued technology including the child having a tantrum. This most often occurred when there was no warning of the ending of a session or when the child was tired.

Typically, technology use was initiated or followed by normal daily routines and home play. This gives the impression that technology is part of everyday life at home and in some cases was the first activity of the day for the child. Parents who did report emotional disturbances for the child prior to technology use (e.g., unsettled behaviour) were then inclined to report technology use as a calming or distraction tool. Parents who reported emotional demands for more technology following a technology session, usually noted shorter technology sessions, however, these emotional disturbances could be due to many different reasons.

One of the other main activities following technology use was sleeping, and most children in the study were going to bed for the night soon after technology use. Technology use by young children has in previous research and in this sample been used as a sleep aid or in bedtime routines, which can affect children's sleep quality (Brown & Smolenaers, 2018; Holloway et al., 2014; Kabali et al., 2015). Using technology close to bedtime or specifically as a sleep aid has been found to negatively impact children's sleep but seems to be a common use of technology with young children. Twenty percent of the children in the study were using technology as part of a bedtime routine which is similar to the findings by RCH (2017) that 29% of pre-schoolers engage in screen-based activity at bedtime%). As previously mentioned, there was a peak in technology use in the late afternoon to evening, with a greater number of instances occurring prior to bed. This suggests using technology within a short time frame before sleep perhaps as a sleep aid, is on the rise. The parent of one child even commented the child took longer to get to sleep following the use of technology.

Conclusion

Previous studies (e.g., Holloway et al., 2013) have highlighted risks and concerns associated with technology use by young children. The findings of the current study as well as in previous studies, have found technology use in children aged between 0- to 6-year-olds to be consistently above recommended governmental guidelines. While much research has focused on the amount of screen time, it is becoming increasingly apparent that developing a better understanding of the function and use of technology in young children is also of great importance (Carson & Janssen, 2012; Holloway et al., 2013; Lauricella et al., 2015).

When considering the findings of this research, it was clear there was enormous variation in the duration of screen time the children experienced. Määttä (2017) has found parent education levels to be associated with lower levels of screen time by preschool age children (3–6 years of age). However, no significant difference was found in the total hours of technology use reported of children in relation to parent education which may be reflective of the sample size. Despite higher parent education levels, the very young children in this study are still partaking in technology use above recommendations—which supports the findings of RCH (2017) and Plowman et al. (2010) that many parents do not tend to place any screen time restrictions on the very young.

The function of technology use of young children needs to be considered. The home environment, family, and parental attitudes. play an important part in influencing technology use. The findings in this study do offer a better understanding into the complex nature of technology use of 0- to 6-year-olds and the way technology is integrated into their home lives. Technology appears to be used primarily as a means of entertainment for children or to provide an opportunity for parents to complete other tasks. However, this finding also means parents are not generally co-viewing or engaging with their child when they use technology or explaining and discussing content to the child to enhance comprehension. Further research is required regarding the function of use, instead of simply focusing on screen time. The home environment as a whole should be considered and factors determining healthy technology use for each family member should be given adequate attention (Canadian Paediatric Society, 2017; Lauricella et al., 2015).

Previous research has suggested that screen time has an adverse effect on development including negatively affecting executive functioning (Canadian Paediatric Society, 2017), language development (Chonchaiya & Pruksananonda, 2008; Lagercrantz, 2016; Plowman et al., 2010), behaviour (Berk, 2006), and attention (Zimmerman & Christakis, 2007). With the great majority of sessions in this research focused on entertainment, the risks associated with early technology use may be heightened. Further research is required focusing on the content young children are viewing to validate these findings: as healthy technology choices for young children should have a focus on prioritising age-appropriate educational or prosocial content (Garrison & Christakis, 2012). However, given that parents are using technology to aid in their household chores, more creative ways to monitor the content children are watching will need to be utilised. A further extension of this type is research is to classify what content is deemed as quality entertainment or education and suitable for healthy viewing.

Limitations, Strengths, and Implications

Like any research, this study also contained some limitations. As is typical for this type of research, the diary completers ($n = 15$) were mostly made up of highly educated mothers (93.30%). Past parenting studies have noted the difficulties in attracting fathers to participate in research (Meunier & Roskam, 2009). Further research would benefit from broader recruitment strategies to attract a wider range of participants.

A strength of this research is the methodology. Too often self-reporting methods are used however diary methods help to minimise the biases from self-reporting methods (Määttä et al., 2017). Advantages of using a diary for this type of research include parents recording experiences as they occur rather than having to remember them later or simply forgetting. Thus, the circumstances surrounding the child using technology and exactly what they are doing is more easily captured, closer to the time they occurred.

The findings of this research, along with previous research have found that technology use in young children is consistently above recommended guidelines. This suggests the next step is the investigation of parental attitudes and knowledge about these recommendations. We propose that screen time is not so much the issue, but perhaps the content and function of technology use should be considered. As suggested by the AAP (2016) the level of screen time is of importance but mainly in conjunction with age, content viewed, and context (i.e., supervised or co-viewing). The home environment, family, and parental attitudes all play an important part in influencing technology use. The findings in this study offer a view into the complex nature of technology use of 0- to 6-year-olds and the way technology is integrated into their home lives.

Appendix A

See Table 1.

Table 1. Code book for content analysis

Diary question analysed	Coding label	Description of activity
Why was this technology used?	1. Entertainment	Used to provide entertainment to the child (e.g., cartoons and movies)
	2. Educational	Programs or apps specifically used for educational purposes
	3. Ready routines	Technology used as part of the child's routines in getting ready for the day
	4. Bedtime routines	Technology used as a distraction, background or focus point for getting the child ready for bed
	5. Parental helper	Technology used as a distraction or to keep the child occupied, with specifically stated reasons for allowing the parent to take time out, complete a task, or assist to calm a child
	6. Incidental watching	Technology viewed because of someone else's use (e.g. siblings technology time)
What was happening just before or when the child accessed the technology?	1. Normal routines	The child was taking part in any activity that is a regular part of the family routine (e.g. having a meal, getting ready for bed, school drop-off)
	2. Formal education	The child attended some form of formal education (e.g. school, pre-school)
	3. Extracurricular activity	The child participated in an external organised activity (e.g. dance classes, a soccer game)
	4. Social interaction	The child was visiting friends or family external to the home

Diary question analysed	Coding label	Description of activity
	5. Home play	Play at home (e.g. indoor or outdoor play)
	6. Emotional	Any emotional response from the child conveyed by the parent as a precursor to technology
	7. Sleeping	The child was asleep immediately prior, whether a night sleep or just a nap
	8. Not enough information	Responses that led to no distinct classification or contained no response
What happened after the technology use was ceased?	1. Normal routines	The child was taking part in any activity as a regular part of the family routine (e.g. having a meal, getting ready for bed, school drop-off)
	2. Formal education	The child attended some form of formal education (e.g. school, pre-school)
	3. Extracurricular activity	The child participated in an external organised activity (e.g. dance classes, a soccer game)
	4. Social Interaction	The child was visiting friends or family external to the home
	5. Home play	Play at home (e.g. indoor or outdoor play)
	6. Emotional or technology demand	Any emotion from the child as a direct consequence of technology use; or pleas for extended use of technology
	7. Sleeping	The child went to sleep immediately following, whether a night sleep or just a nap
	8. Not enough information	Responses that led to no distinct classification or no response

References

American Academy of Pediatrics. (2016). *American Academy of Pediatrics announces new recommendations for children's media use*. Retrieved from https://www.aap.org/en-us/about-the-aap/aap-press-room/Pages/American-Academy-of-Pediatrics-Announces-New-Recommendations-for-Childrens-Media-Use.aspx

Australia Bureau of Statistics. (2018). *Household use of information technology, Australia, 2016–17*. Retrieved from http://www.abs.gov.au/AUSSTATS/abs@.nsf/allprimarymainfeatures/ACC2D18CC958BC7BCA2568A9001393AE?opendocument

Australian Bureau of Statistics. (2012). *Children's participation in cultural and leisure activities, Australia, April 2012*. Retrieved from http://www.abs.gov.au/ausstats/abs@.nsf/Products/4901.0~Apr+2012~Main+Features~Internet+and+mobile+phones?OpenDocument

Barr, R., Lauricella, A., Zack, E., & Calvert, S. L. (2010). Infant and early childhood exposure to adult-directed and child-directed television programming. *Merrill-Palmer Quarterly, 56*, 21–48.

Berk, L. (2006). *Child development* (7th ed.). Pearson Education.

Brown, A., & Smolenaers, E. (2018). Parents' interpretations of screen time recommendations for children younger than 2 years. *Journal of Family Issues, 39*, 406–429.

Canadian Paediatric Society. (2017). Screen time and young children: Promoting health and development in a digital world. *Paediatrics & Child Health, 22*, 461–468.

Canadian Paediatric Society, Digital Health Task Force, Ottawa, Ontario. (2019). Digital media: Promoting healthy screen use in school-aged children and adolescents. *Paediatrics & Child Health, 24*(6), 402–408.

Chonchaiya, W., & Pruksananonda, C. (2008). Television viewing associates with delayed language development. *Acta Paediatrica, 97*, 977–982.

Cliff, D. P., Howard, S. J., Radesky, J. S., McNeill, J., & Vella, S. A. (2018). Early childhood media exposure and self-regulation: Bi-directional longitudinal associations. *Academic Pediatrics, 18*, 813–819.

DeCuir-Gunby, J. T., Marshall, P. L., & McCulloch, A. W. (2011). Developing and using a codebook for the analysis of interview data: An example from a professional development research project. *Field Methods, 23*(2), 136–155.

Department of Health and Aging. (2018). *National physical activity recommendations for children (0–5 years)*. Retrieved from https://www.10000steps.org.au/articles/national-physical-activity-recommendations-children-0-5-years/

Ferguson, C. J., & Donnellan, M. B. (2014). Is the association between children's baby video viewing and poor language developement robust? A reanalysis of Zimmerman, Christakis, and Meltzoff (2007). *Developmental Psychology, 50*(1), 129–137. https://doi.org/10.1037/a0033628

Holloway, D., Green L., & Livingstone, S. (2010). *Zero to eight: Young children and their internet use.* EU Kids Online.
Holloway, D., Green L., & Livingstone, S. (2013). *Zero to eight: Young children and their internet use.* LSE: EU Kids Online.
Huber, B., Yeates, M., Meyer, D., Fleckhammer, L., & Kaufman, J. (2018). The effects of screen media content on young children's executive functioning. *Journal of Experimental Child Psychology, 170,* 72–85.
Johnson, G. M., & Puplampu, K. P. (2008). Internet use during childhood and the ecological techno-subsystem. *Canadian Journal of Learning and Technology/La Revue Canadienne de L'apprentissage et de La Technologie, 34*(1). https://doi.org/10.21432/T2CP4T
Kabali, H. K., Irigoyen, M. M., Nunez-Davis R., Budacki, J. G., Mohanty, S. H., Leister, K. P., & Bonner, R. L. (2015). Exposure and use of mobile media devices by young children. *Pediatrics, 136,* 1044–1050.
Krippendorff, K. (2004). *Content analysis: An introduction to its methodology* (2nd ed.). Sage Publications Inc.
Lagercrantz, H. (2016). Connecting the brain of the child from synapses to screen-based activity. *Acta Paediatrica, 105,* 352–357.
Lauricella, A. R., Wartella, E., & Rideout, V. J. (2015). Young children's screen time: The complex role of parent and child factors. *Journal of Applied Developmental Psychology, 36,* 11–17.
Lombard, M., Snyder-Duch, J., & Bracken, C. C. (2002). Content analysis in mass communication: Assessment and reporting of intercoder reliability. *Human Communication Research, 28,* 587–604.
Määttä S., Kaukonen R., Vepsäläinen, H., Lehto, E., Ylönen, A., Ray, C., Erkkola M., & Roos, E. (2017). The mediating role of the home environment in relation to parental educational level and preschool children's screen time: A cross-sectional study. *BMC Public Health, 17.*
Madigan, S., McArthur, B. A., Anjorn, C., Eirich, R., & Christakis, D. A. (2020). Associations between screen use and child language skills. *JAMA Pediatrics, 174*(7), 1–11. https://doi.org/10.1001/jamapediatrics.2020.0327
Plowman, L., McPake, J., & Stephen, C. (2010). The technologisation of childhood? Young children and technology in the home. *Children and Society, 24,* 63–74.
Royal Children's Hospital Melbourne. (2017). *Screen time and kids: What's happening in our homes?* Retrieved from https://www.rchpoll.org.au/wp-content/uploads/2017/06/ACHP-Poll7_Detailed-Report-June21.pdf
Wartella, E., Richert, R. A., & Robb, M. B. (2010). Babies, television and videos: How did we get here? *Developmental Review, 30,* 116–127.

World Health Organization. (2019) . *Guidelines on physical activity, sedentary behaviour and sleep for children under 5 years of age*. World Health Organization. https://apps.who.int/iris/handle/10665/311664 License: CC BYNC-SA 3.0 IGO.

Zimmerman, F. J., & Christakis, D. A. (2007). Associations between content types of early media exposure and subsequent attentional problems. *Pediatrics, 120*, 986–992.

Talkin' Bout My Generation: The Utility of Different Age Cohorts to Predict Antisocial Behaviour on Social Media

Molly Branson, Evita March, and Jessica Z. Marrington

Abstract Experiencing antisocial online behaviour such as cyberbullying and internet trolling is associated with a range of negative psychological and physical outcomes. To understand why people are motivated to engage in antisocial online behaviour, researchers have explored a variety of individual differences including traits, motivations, and cognitions. In the current study, we adopted developmental frameworks to explore antisocial use of social media across different age cohorts. Participants ($N = 665$, 51% female) with an average age of 28 years ($SD = 8.86$) completed an online questionnaire assessing antisocial use of social media. Adopting previous guidelines, participants were categorised as emerging adults (aged 18–25 years; 50%), adults (aged 26–44 years; 42%), and middle age (aged 45–59 years; 8%). A one-way ANOVA showed a statistically significant effect of age cohort on antisocial use;

M. Branson · E. March (✉)
Federation University Australia, Berwick, Australia
e-mail: e.march@federation.edu.au

J. Z. Marrington
University of Southern Queensland, Ipswich, Australia

however, contrary to expectations, adults reported higher antisocial use of social media compared to emerging adults and middle-aged adults. There was no statistically significant difference between emerging adults and middle-aged adults. Results are discussed through the lens of Erikson's psychosocial theory and Social Convoy Model and recommendations are provided to manage and prevent perpetration of antisocial online behaviour.

Keywords Development · Adolescent · Adult · Online · Antisocial · Motives

Social media has long been considered the domain of the young, with emerging adults and adolescents generally participating in online social media activity more frequently and in greater volume when compared to older generations (Barnhart, 2021). Still, recent data illustrates a considerable increase in the number of adults age 30 and above using social media (Pew Research Centre, 2019). Although recent estimates show 71% of Australian adults regularly use social media (Barnhart, 2021), researchers have typically neglected to explore the online behaviour of different age groups, largely focusing on the online behaviour of adolescent and emerging adult populations (for a meta-analytic review, see Kowalski et al., 2014). In the current study, we attempt to address this paucity in the literature by exploring online behaviour across different age groups. Specifically, we explore antisocial online behaviour.

Antisocial Online Behaviour

Although social media allows for increased interpersonal interaction (Subramanian, 2017), these interpersonal interactions are not always positive. Antisocial interpersonal behaviours experienced online include cyberbullying (i.e., willful and repeated harm inflicted via electronic devices; Hinduja & Patchin, 2014), trolling (i.e., deliberately provoking, disrupting, and upsetting others; March & Steele, 2020; March, 2019) and cyberstalking (i.e., willful, repeated, and malicious following, harassment, or sabotage of another person in online contexts; Sheridan & Grant, 2007). Experiencing antisocial online behaviour has negative physiological and psychological outcomes, including substance abuse, anxiety, depression, poor physical health, and self-injury (see Kowalski et al., 2014).

Research exploring perpetration of antisocial online behaviour (namely cyberbullying) has predominantly explored adolescent populations (for a metanalytic review, see Kowalski et al., 2014). Perpetration of antisocial online behaviour has been shown to increase throughout adolescence, with peak perpetration rates (~40–50%; Ševčíková & Šmahel, 2009) occurring during emerging adulthood (Bartlett & Chamberlain, 2017). However, recent figures indicate that the behaviour does not cease at adulthood (Ferenczi et al., 2017; Ševčíková & Šmahel, 2009). Although these behaviours do not cease, the trend does appear to reverse as adults age. Of the limited studies that have explored adult populations, negative associations have been identified between age and cyberbullying perpetration (Bartlett & Chamberlain, 2017; Gibb & Devereux, 2014), age and trolling behaviours (Craker & March, 2016), and age and antisocial use of Facebook (Ferenczi et al., 2017). When taken together, these findings indicate perpetration of antisocial online behaviour is most prevalent in emerging adulthood with the incidence of perpetration reducing with age. To date, however, researchers have not yet directly compared this perpetration across the different age groups.

To evaluate the differences between age groups, we adopt age-cohort guidelines recently implemented by Peng et al. (2020). Using these guidelines, we refer to three age ranges/cohorts corresponding to a distinct stage of psychosocial development. In line with Peng et al. (2020), we use the term 'emerging adults' to refer to participants aged 18–25 years, 'adults' to refer to participants aged 26–44 years, and 'middle-age adults' to refer to participants aged 45–59 years.

Antisocial Online Behaviour and Age: A Theoretical Framework

To explain the relationship between age and perpetrating antisocial online behaviour, we appeal to Erikson's (1959) model of psychosocial development, which outlines lifetime developmental stages with each stage involving a developmental 'crisis' to resolve. According to Erikson's psychosocial model, the adolescent stage of identity versus role confusion involves the synthesis or confusion of identity via antisocial or prosocial relationships (Erikson, 1959; Newman & Newman, 2017).

Although Erikson initially proposed that this identity crisis occurred during adolescence, neo-psychosocial theorists (i.e., Marcia et al., 2012) have proposed the continuation of this stage into emerging adulthood, and researchers have confirmed that emerging adults typically continue exploring and experimenting with their identity (Newman & Newman, 2017). Following synthesis (or otherwise) of this stage, adults progress to the stage of intimacy versus isolation (Erikson, 1959), wherein they tend to seek intimate relationships and meaning through childbearing, work, and lifestyle milestones (Newman & Newman, 2017). Progression through this stage then leads to the psychosocial stage of middle age, which involves the crisis of generativity versus stagnation (Erikson, 1959). Within this stage, middle-aged adults seek to 'leave their mark' on the world through the focus and nurture involved with family relationships (Erikson, 1959).

We consider Erikson's theory of psychosocial development to be an appropriate model to apply to age and antisocial online behaviour. Emerging adults who are in the identification stage typically place increased importance on social relationships (Erikson, 1959), and are more susceptible to influence from online relationships, which may lead them to engage in antisocial online behaviour such as cyberbullying (Cho & Yoo, 2017). Further, social comparison, which plays a particularly important role in identity (Ragelienė, 2016), has been found to predict perpetration of antisocial online behaviour (Young et al., 2017). Emerging adults also tend to have increased numbers of 'friends' on social media when compared to their older counterparts (Quinn et al., 2013), which is also associated with increased perpetration of antisocial online behaviour (Young et al., 2017). Combined, these results support the rationale to expect emerging adults to engage in increased perpetration of antisocial online behaviour.

Upon transitioning from this identification stage, individuals (now adults) enter the intimacy stage, where they turn their attentions towards seeking intimate, loving relationships, attending to these relationships in order to deter loneliness and isolation (Malone et al., 2016; Newman & Newman, 2017). In this age group, we rationalise that it would be likely for these adults to use social media to pursue intimacy and meaning in their interpersonal online interactions. Based on this supposition, these adults would be less likely to behave antisocially online, as doing so would result in isolation and loneliness rather than intimate, meaningful relationships.

In middle age, adults are typically in the generativity psychosocial stage, where they tend to nurture and care for their social relationships (Newman & Newman, 2017), and make positive changes that benefit other people (Malone et al., 2016). Based on this motivation to make positive connections with others and leave a lasting positive 'imprint' on the world, it seems unlikely that these individuals would behave antisocially online. This psychosocial stage is personified by engagement in prosocial behaviours and interactions (Wenner & Randall, 2016), Thus, it is unlikely that middle-aged adults would use social media antisocially. In sum, appealing to Erikson's theory indicates that of the three age cohorts of emerging adult, adult, and middle-age adult, emerging adults are more likely to behave antisocially online.

In addition to Erikson's theory of psychosocial development, we also appeal to Social Convoy Model (Antonucci et al., 2014) to understand age cohorts and antisocial online behaviour. According to Social Convoy Model, our social groups (i.e., convoys) vary in quality (i.e., positive or negative), function (i.e., aid, affect), and structure (i.e., size, composition, frequency of contact), and these convoys are influenced by situation and personal characteristics, such as age (Antonucci et al., 2014). For example, middle-aged adults keep a closer, more supportive convoy of people in proximity to themselves, often composed of younger people who are related to the individual (i.e., family members, children, and grandchildren; Antonucci et al., 2014). Because of the nature (positive) and function (aid/ support), of these convoys, middle-aged adults may be less likely to conduct themselves antisocially. Indeed, research indicates that older social media users tend to have smaller circles of online friends, and have more positive, prosocial experiences online (Quinn et al., 2016). By contrast, younger adults tend to have more extensive circles of friends and less family friends in their support networks (Levitt et al., 1993). The reliance on friends rather than family for affirmation and support may result in using social media as a mechanism to affirm social status among one's peers through antisocial behaviours (i.e., cyberbullying). This, according to this model, the social convoys of younger adults, comparative to older adults, may influence them to behave more antisocially.

The Current Study

Although much of the existing research evaluating the perpetration of antisocial online behaviours has utilised adolescent samples (for a review, see Kowalski et al., 2014), recent figures indicate that the behaviour does not cease at adulthood (Ferenczi et al., 2017; Ševčíková & Šmahel, 2009). Despite this, relatively few studies have investigated the effect of age cohorts on perpetration of antisocial online behaviour. In the current study, we explored antisocial use of social media across different age groups: Emerging adults (aged 18–25), adults (aged 26–44), and middle-aged adults (45–59 years). To explore these age cohorts, we appeal to Erikson's (1959) psychosocial theory of development and the Social Convoy Model (Antonucci et al., 2014). Based on these theories, it is likely that younger age cohorts will be the most likely to use social media for antisocial purposes.

The aim of this study was to explore the effect of age cohorts on antisocial use of social media. Based on previous research (Ferenczi et al., 2017; Gibb & Devereux, 2014; Quinn et al., 2013), psychosocial theory, and Social Convoy Model of interpersonal development, it was predicted that there will be a significant effect of age cohorts on antisocial use of social media. Specifically, the cohort of emerging adults (age 18–25 years) will be more likely to use social media antisocially compared to the cohorts of adults (age 26–44 years) and older adults (age 45–59 years).

Method

Participants

Participants were a community sample ($N = 655$) with 51.8% women and 48.2% men. Participants age ranged from 18 to 59 years, with an average age of 28 years ($SD = 8.87$), and predominantly resided in Australia (75.4%), the United States (10.1%), and the United Kingdom (4.2%). Following previous research guidelines (see Peng et al., 2020), participants were categorised into the following age cohorts: Emerging adults (18–25 years), adults (26–44 years), and middle-age adults (45–59 years). Of the sample, 50.1% ($N = 333$) were emerging adults, 42.1% ($N = 280$) were adults, and 7.8% ($N = 52$) were middle-age adults. Per day, emerging adults spent an average 7.67 hours ($SD = 3.33$) on the Internet and 3.89 hours ($SD = 2.73$) on social media.

Adults spent an average 8.39 hours ($SD = 3.86$) on the Internet and 4.41 hours ($SD = 2.69$) on social media. Middle-age adults spent an average 5.81 hours ($SD = 3.96$) on the Internet and 2.52 hours ($SD = 2.11$) on social media.

Measures

Age, country of residence, and questions related to internet and social media use were measured with a basic demographic questionnaire. Antisocial use of social media was measured with a modified version of the Uses of Facebook Scale (Ferenczi et al., 2017). The Uses of Facebook Scale includes two subscales: Antisocial uses and prosocial uses. In the current study, only the antisocial uses subscale (7-items) was included. To assess social media in general, the term 'Facebook' was modified to 'social media'. For example, the item 'I use Facebook to badmouth people' was modified to read 'I use social media to badmouth people', and the item 'I use Facebook to show off' was modified to read 'I use social media to show off'. Participants responded to items on a 7-point Likert scale ($1 =$ *Strongly Disagree*, $7 =$ *Strongly Agree*) and internal consistency was acceptable (Cronbach's alpha $= 0.76$).

Procedure

After receiving relevant institution Human Research Ethics Committee approval, participants were recruited via social media advertising and snowballing techniques. Advertisements on social media invited participants to participate in a voluntary, and anonymous online questionnaire. Upon completion, participants were thanked and data were downloaded for analyses.

Design

The design of the study was cross-sectional and quasi-experimental, with one Independent Variable (IV; age cohort) with three levels (emerging adults, adults, middle-age adults), and one Dependent Variable (DV; antisocial use of social media).

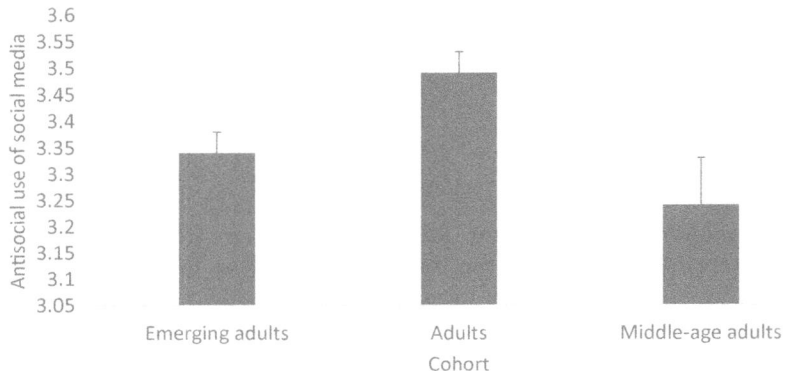

Fig. 1 Mean differences for age cohorts and antisocial use of social media. Error bars represent Standard Error

Results

Before running the analysis, the assumption of normality was checked via histogram and was significantly positively skewed. As such, a square root transformation was applied to the dependent variable, which mildly corrected the skew. Although a minor skew was still present, given the robustness of the F test to minor violations of normality (Keppel & Wickens, 2004), we proceeded with data analysis. A one-way ANOVA indicated a significant effect of age cohort on antisocial use of social media, $F(2,662) = 4.84$, $p = .008$, with a small effect of $\eta_p^2 = 0.01$. Post-hoc tests with a Tukey's HSD correction indicated that adults' antisocial use was significantly higher than emerging adults' antisocial use (see Fig. 1), $p = .025$. In addition, adults' antisocial use was significantly higher than middle-age adults' antisocial use, $p = .046$. There was no significant difference between emerging adults' antisocial use and middle-age adults' antisocial use.

DISCUSSION

The aim of this study was to determine the effect of age cohort (emerging adults, adults, and middle-aged adults) on antisocial use of social media. In support of our hypothesis, antisocial use of social media varied according to age cohort. Contrary to our predictions, however, adults (aged 26–44 years) were significantly more likely to use social media antisocially when compared to emerging adults (aged 18–25 years) and middle-aged adults (aged 45–59 years). There was no significant difference found between emerging and middle-aged adults.

The tendency for adults to engage in more antisocial social media behaviour compared to young and middle-aged adults is in contrast to findings of previous research, with consistent reports that young adults are more likely to engage in antisocial online behaviours when compared to older adults (Barlett & Chamberlin, 2017; Ferenczi et al., 2017; Gibb & Devereux, 2014). To consider possible explanations for this surprising result, we return to Erikson's (1959) theory. Psychosocially speaking, Erikson proposes that the developmental stage associated with emerging adulthood involves a period within which social interaction and influence encourage identity formation and synthesis. Indeed, because this developmental stage is associated with increased importance placed on social relationships (Erikson, 1959), it follows that emerging adults are likely to use social media with the intention of enhancing their social status through online social interaction (Barker, 2012). Because social comparison and social status affirmation have both been proposed as motivators of antisocial online behaviours (Patchin & Hinduja, 2012; Young et al., 2017), it was expected that emerging adults would be more likely than older adults to engage in antisocial behaviour online. However, the results of the current study appear to indicate that this may not be true. As this study is the first to explore age cohorts and antisocial online behaviour, interpretation is somewhat speculative. Still, it is possible that the importance of social influence on emerging adult's identity experimentation may reduce their likelihood of using social media antisocially. Due to the importance placed on social relationships during this developmental stage, the perpetration of antisocial online behaviours may actually harm the social status of emerging adults, possibly resulting in disapproval from their all-important social circles. In fact, results of the current study potentially corroborate findings that emerging adults tend to be particularly concerned about their self-presentation on social media (Yang et al., 2017), and seek to craft an online identity that allows them to both maintain existing offline relationships (Stephenson-Abetz & Holman, 2012) while also creating new online connections (Yang, 2018). Therefore, to maintain and develop social relationships online, emerging adults might engage in less antisocial online behaviour.

Unexpectedly, and in contrast to the hypothesis, adults (age 26–44) were more likely to use social media antisocially compared to emerging and middle-age adults. This finding contradicts previous research exploring age differences in antisocial online behaviour, which has found that these behaviours become less frequent as adults age (Bartlett & Chamberlain, 2017; Ferenczi et al., 2017; Gibb & Devereux, 2014). To explain this unexpected finding, we again appeal to Erikson's psychosocial theory. We speculate that this finding may be reflective of the psychosocial crisis associated with this age period; according to Erikson's theory, during this age individuals seek to form and maintain close, intimate relationships (Newman & Newman, 2017). Social media's broad, expansive friend circles which are typically associated with reduced intimacy (Sutcliffe et al., 2018), may be counter-intuitive to the developmental 'needs' of this stage. Because the social interactions on social networking sites reflect a broad range of social relationships (i.e., not just close, personal relationships, but also extended 'acquaintance' relationships), it is plausible that adults may be more inclined to behave antisocially, due to the lack of consequence that would otherwise be associated with directing the behaviour towards a close/intimate friend or family member.

As expected, middle-aged adults (aged 45–59) were less likely to use social media for antisocial purposes. This finding supports previous research indicating a negative relationship between age and antisocial use of social media (Bartlett & Chamberlain, 2017; Craker & March, 2016; Ferenczi et al., 2017; Gibb & Devereux, 2014), and can be interpreted in terms of the associated Eriksonian psychosocial developmental stage. Because adults of this stage have a tendency to not only nurture personal relationships, but also harness a desire to leave lasting positive traces on the world (Erikson, 1959), it is possible that middle-age adults would be unlikely to utilise social media for antisocial purposes, as doing so would likely prevent the desired generativity associated with this stage.

The finding that antisocial use of social media peaks during adulthood (26–44) before decreasing in middle age can also be interpreted within the Social Convoy Model. Although adults were the most likely to use social media antisocially compared to the other age cohorts, it is possible that their significance emerged as a comparison to the relatively reduced levels associated with the emerging and middle-aged groups. To clarify, emerging adults are more likely to emphasise the importance of social relationships, and tend to have more 'friends' on social media platforms than older adults (Quinn et al., 2016). It was hypothesised that this reliance on social relationships (i.e., convoys) would result in a desire to affirm social status and, by extension, antisocial online behaviour. However, it is possible these extensive online social 'convoys', may actually deter such behaviour, with the social quality (positive) and function (social status) discouraging antisocial behaviour among convoy members. Similarly, although the online convoys in which middle-aged adults function tend to be smaller in number (Quinn et al., 2016), members of this age cohort are likely to place similar importance and emphasis on their online relationships. Indeed, middle-aged adults' social convoys tend to be supportive in function, often composed of family members and more intimate others (Antonucci et al., 2014). It therefore follows that, because of the positive nature of the typical 'convoys' associated with the emerging and middle-aged adult cohorts, it is unlikely that these cohorts would participate in antisocial online behaviour.

Implications

The findings of the current study regarding age and antisocial use of social media have numerous implications. The differences identified between the age cohorts highlight the need for further research exploring the online behaviour of different age cohorts. Much research evaluating antisocial behaviour online has focused on adolescent/young adult populations samples (Kowalski et al., 2014), a possible artefact of the presumption that these behaviours are more prevalent in younger people. Our findings emphasise the importance of evaluating antisocial online behaviours among broader age demographics.

In addition to research sampling implications, results of the current study can also inform social media policies and procedures. For example, Facebook's 'Put a Stop to Bullying' campaign has predominantly campaigned for a reduction in antisocial behaviour on the platform among adolescents (Facebook, 2022). Our findings indicate the potential short-sightedness of this campaign; such tunnel vision that neglects exploring antisocial online behaviour in other age cohorts could potentially be detrimental to social media users. Based on results of the current study, social media such as Facebook should seek to re-examine their community guidelines and safety campaigns to include behaviour in adult populations. This, in turn, may result in greater awareness and more focused policing, thereby reducing the occurrence of the harm caused by these behaviours.

Limitations, Future Directions, and Conclusions

A number of limitations of the current study should be considered. Although the age cohorts included in this study were based on previously identified guidelines (e.g., Peng et al., 2020), it is possible that the age variance in our designated cohorts may have undermined the specificity of the results. For example, some researchers have proposed that adulthood (which we defined as being 26–44), is actually comprised of multiple stages of psychosocial development (Newman & Newman, 2017). As such, in order to gain a more specific understanding of the effect of age cohorts on antisocial social media use, future research should seek to break down this age cohort into smaller groups in order to get a more nuanced understanding as to how age and level of psychosocial development relate to antisocial online behaviour.

It is also worthwhile considering that in the current study, we explored antisocial online behaviours as a catchall construct, whereas previous research has explored specific antisocial behaviours such as cyberbullying and trolling. It is possible that the unexpected results of the current study are a product of exploring antisocial online behaviours as an overall behaviour instead of specific antisocial online behaviours. We recommend that future research seek to explore these age groups and perpetration of these specific antisocial online behaviours (i.e., cyberbullying, trolling). Further, future researchers might explore age cohorts across other behaviour online, such as prosocial online behaviour (March & Marrington, 2021) and authentic self-presentation (Geary et al., 2021).

Furthermore, although the Uses of Facebook Scale (Ferenczi et al., 2017) demonstrated good internal consistency, the scale's items are somewhat limited in their content. Although the scale's wording was modified to reflect 'social media' rather than Facebook specifically, the behaviours included in the items may not accurately capture behaviour on social media. For example, research indicates that significant differences exist in users' motivations to use different social media sites (Alhabash & Ma, 2017). Due to these differences, future research should seek to conduct age-cohort research with platform specific scales, evaluating the occurrence of behaviours common to that specific networking site. A mixed methods approach may also offer additional insight into antisocial behaviours online. Because self-report measures can be subject to biased responses, qualitative or mixed research may be better able to elucidate the relationship between age and antisocial online behaviour.

For example, cross-referencing participants' social media pages to their self-report responses may illuminate any malingering, thereby producing a more nuanced, accurate portrayal of participants' online habits.

As social media has become an increasingly important mechanism for social communication, the manifestation of antisocial behaviours on social media platforms has become more prevalent. Because these antisocial behaviours have numerous psychological and physiological consequences to victims (Kowalski et al., 2014), it is important to gain a greater understanding of why these behaviours occur in order to prevent future occurrence. Largely, previous research has explored antisocial online behaviour in younger populations (see Kowalski et al., 2014). In the current study, we explored, for the first time, the effect of age cohorts on antisocial use of social media. Contrary to expectations, adults, not emerging adults or middle-age adults, were the most likely to use social media antisocially. We posit that this finding may be indicative of the psychosocial developmental stage associated with adulthood and relevant social convoys. Future research should seek to replicate these findings with alternative, sensitive measurement, and more refined cohorts to allow for more specific perpetrator profiling and, inevitably, prevention of these behaviours.

References

Alhabash, S., & Ma, M. (2017). A tale of four platforms: Motivations and uses of Facebook, Twitter, Instagram, and Snapchat among college students? *Social Media + Society*, 3(1), 205630511769154. https://doi.org/10.1177/2056305117691544

Antonucci, T. C., Ajrouch, K. J., & Birditt, K. S. (2014). The convoy model: Explaining social relations from a multidisciplinary perspective. *The Gerontologist*, 54(1), 82–92. https://doi.org/10.1093/geront/gnt118

Barker, V. (2012). A generational comparison of social networking site use: The influence of age and social identity. *The International Journal of Aging and Human Development*, 74(2), 163–187. https://doi.org/10.2190%2FAG.74.2.d

Barnhart, B. (2021, March 9). *Social media demographics to inform your brand's strategy in 2021*. Sprout Social. https://sproutsocial.com/insights/new-social-media-demographics/

Bartlett, C. P., & Chamberlin, K. (2017). Examining cyberbullying across the lifespan. *Computers in Human Behavior*, 71, 444–449. https://doi.org/10.1016/j.chb.2017.02.009

Cho, Y. K., & Yoo, J. W. (2017). Cyberbullying, internet and SNS usage types, and perceived social support: A comparison of different age groups. *Information, Communication & Society, 20*(10), 1464–1481. https://doi.org/10.1080/1369118X.2016.1228998

Craker, N., & March, E. (2016). The dark side of Facebook®: The Dark Tetrad, negative social potency, and trolling behaviours. *Personality and Individual Differences, 102*, 79–84. https://doi.org/10.1016/j.paid.2016.06.043

Erikson, E. H. (1959). *Identity and the life cycle: Selected papers*. International Universities Press.

Facebook (2022). *Put a stop to bullying*. Retrieved March 1, 2020, from https://www.facebook.com/safety/bullying

Ferenczi, N., Marshall, T. C., & Bejanyan, K. (2017). Are sex differences in antisocial and prosocial Facebook use explained by narcissism and relational self-construal? *Computers in Human Behavior, 77*, 25–31. https://doi.org/10.1016/j.chb.2017.08.033

Geary, C., March, E., & Grieve, R. (2021). Insta-identity: Dark personality traits as predictors of authentic self-presentation on Instagram. *Telematics and Informatics, 63*, 101669. https://doi.org/10.1016/j.tele.2021.101669

Gibb, Z. G., & Devereux, P. G. (2014). Who does that anyway? Predictors and personality correlates of cyberbullying in college. *Computers in Human Behavior, 38*, 8–16. https://doi.org/10.1016/j.chb.2014.05.009

Hinduja, S., & Patchin, J. W. (2014). *Bullying beyond the schoolyard: Preventing and responding to cyberbullying*. Corwin Press.

Keppel, G., & Wickens, T. D. (2004). *Design and analysis: A researcher's handbook*. Upper Saddle River.

Kowalski, R. M., Giumetti, G. W., Schroeder, A. N., & Lattanner, M. R. (2014). Bullying in the digital age: A critical review and meta-analysis of cyberbullying research among youth. *Psychological Bulletin, 140*(4), 1073. https://doi.org/10.1037/a0035618

Levitt, M. J., Guacci, N., & Levitt, J. L. (1993). Convoys of social support in childhood and early adolescence: Structure and function. *Developmental Psychology, 29*(5), 811–818. https://doi.org/10.1037/0012-1649.29.5.811

Malone, J. C., Liu, S. R., Vaillant, G. E., Rentz, D. M., & Waldinger, R. J. (2016). Midlife Eriksonian psychosocial development: Setting the stage for late-life cognitive and emotional health. *Developmental Psychology, 52*(3), 496–508. https://doi.org/10.1037/a0039875

March, E., & Marrington, J. Z. (2021). Antisocial and prosocial online behaviour: Exploring the roles of the dark and light triads. *Current Psychology*, 1–4. https://doi.org/10.1007/s12144-021-01552-7

March, E., & Steele, G. (2020). High esteem and hurting others online: Trait sadism moderates the relationship between selfesteem and Internet trolling.

Cyberpsychology, Behavior, and Social Networking, 23(7), 441–446. https://doi.org/10.1089/cyber.2019.0652

Marcia, J. E., Waterman, A. S., Matteson, D. R., Archer, S. L., & Orlofsky, J. L. (2012). *Ego identity: A handbook for psychosocial research*. Springer Science & Business Media

Newman, B. M., & Newman, P. R. (2017). *Development through life: A psychosocial approach*. Cengage Learning.

Patchin, J. W., & Hinduja, S. (2012). Cyberbullying: An update and synthesis of the research. In J. W. Patchin & S. Hinduja (Eds.), *Cyberbullying prevention and response: Expert perspectives* (pp. 13–36). Routledge.

Peng, Y., Zhu, Q., Wang, B., & Ren, J. (2020). A cross-sectional study on interference control: Age affects reactive control but not proactive control. *PeerJ, 8*, 1–14. https://doi.org/10.7717/peerj.8365

Pew Research Center. (2019). *Social media fact sheet*. https://www.pewresearch.org/internet/fact-sheet/social-media/

Quinn, D., Chen, L., & Mulvenna, M. (2013). Discovering social behaviour variances of younger and older users through social interaction analysis. *International Journal of Web Science, 2*(1–2), 44–65. https://doi.org/10.1504/IJWS.2013.056574

Quinn, D., Chen, L., Mulvenna, M. D., & Bond, R. (2016). Exploring the relationship between online social network site usage and the impact on quality of life for older and younger users: An interaction analysis. *Journal of Medical Internet Research, 18*(9), e245. https://doi.org/10.2196/jmir.5377

Ragelienė, T. (2016). Links of adolescents identity development and relationship with peers: A systematic literature review. *Journal of the Canadian Academy of Child and Adolescent Psychiatry, 25*, 97–105.

Ševčíková, A., & Šmahel, D. (2009). Online harassment and cyberbullying in the Czech Republic: Comparison across age groups. *Zeitschrift für Psychologie/Journal of Psychology, 217*(4), 227. https://doi/10.1027/0044-3409.217.4.227

Sheridan, L. P., & Grant, T. (2007). Is cyberstalking different? *Psychology, Crime & Law, 13*(6), 627–640. https://doi.org/10.1080/10683160701340528

Stephenson--Abetz, J., & Holman, A. (2012). Home is where the heart is: Facebook and the negotiation of "old" and "new" during the transition to college. *Western Journal of Communication, 76*(2), 175–193. https://doi.org/10.1080/10570314.2011.654309

Subramanian, K. R. (2017). Influence of social media in interpersonal communication. *International Journal of Scientific Progress and Research, 38*(2), 70–75.

Sutcliffe, A. G., Binder, J. F., & Dunbar, R. I. (2018). Activity in social media and intimacy in social relationships. *Computers in Human Behavior, 85*, 227–235.

Wenner, J. R., & Randall, B. A. (2016). Predictors of prosocial behavior: Differences in middle aged and older adults. *Personality and Individual Differences, 101*, 322–326. https://doi.org/10.1016/j.paid.2016.05.367

Yang, C. (2018). Social media as more than a peer space: College freshmen encountering parents on Facebook. *Journal of Adolescent Research, 33*(4), 442–469. https://doi.org/10.1177/0743558416659750

Yang, C. C., Holden, S. M., & Carter, M. D. (2017). Emerging adults' social media self-presentation and identity development at college transition: Mindfulness as a moderator. *Journal of Applied Developmental Psychology, 52*, 212–221. https://doi.org/10.1016/j.appdev.2017.08.006

Young, R., Len-Ríos, M., & Young, H. (2017). Romantic motivations for social media use, social comparison, and online aggression among adolescents. *Computers in Human Behavior, 75*, 385–395. https://doi-org.ezproxy.federation.edu.au/10.1016/j.chb.2017.04.021

The Impact of Ease of Online Self-Expression During Adolescence on Identity in Young Adulthood

Jaimee Stuart, Riley Scott, Karlee O'Donnell, and Paul E. Jose

Abstract For many young adults today, omnipresent access to and use of digital technologies has formed a core feature of their identity development. However, little research has examined whether attitudes toward engagement with digital technologies during adolescence impact on identity in young adulthood. Using a longitudinal path modeling approach, the current study sought to examine the impacts of online self-expression during adolescence on identity (confusion and confidence), as mediated by peer connectedness. Furthermore, we investigated whether these effects persisted over time to influence identity

---

J. Stuart (✉) · R. Scott · K. O'Donnell
School of Applied Psychology, Griffith University, Brisbane and Gold Coast, QLD, Australia
e-mail: j.stuart@griffith.edu.au

K. O'Donnell
Gold Coast, QLD, Australia

P. E. Jose
School of Psychology, Victoria University of Wellington, Wellington, New Zealand

© The Author(s), under exclusive license to Springer Nature Switzerland AG 2022
T. Machin et al. (eds.), *Social Media and Technology Across the Lifespan*, Palgrave Studies in Cyberpsychology,
https://doi.org/10.1007/978-3-030-99049-7_4

outcomes in emerging adulthood. Data were drawn from the final two waves of the New Zealand Youth Connectedness Project. Adolescent data was collected from 1,809 youth between the ages of 13 and 18 during 2008, and the emerging adult data were collected five years later during 2013 when participants were aged 18–23 years old. Only those who had regular access to the internet ($N = 1233$) during adolescence were included in the analyses. Key results of the longitudinal serial mediation model include that ease of online self-expression in adolescence was directly associated with higher levels of identity confusion. However, the ease of online self-expression was also cross-sectionally associated with lower levels of identity confusion and higher levels of confidence via a stronger sense of peer connectedness. Further, the ease of online self-expression was indirectly associated with greater confidence and lower identity confusion in emerging adulthood via peer connectedness, confidence, and identity confusion in adolescence. These findings suggest that online self-expression during adolescence may be a double-edged sword in that it increases identity confusion but also provides opportunities for connection in ways that promote identity consolidation (increased confidence and reduced confusion).

Keywords Online self-expression · Adolescence · Identity confusion · Self esteem · Peer relationships

Over twenty years ago it was suggested the omnipresence of digital technologies across all spheres of life would result in distinct forms of socialization that would differentiate the learning styles, attention spans, and even brain structures of a new generation of young people (Prenksy, 2001). While subsequent research has found little empirical support for such major divergences in development as a result of technology (Evans & Robertson, 2020), many studies have indicated that youth tend to be more proficient and active users of digital technologies as compared to other age groups (e.g., Helsper & Eynon, 2010). In fact, research has consistently found young people are the largest adopters of new digital technologies, report the greatest frequency of use, and have the highest frequency of technologically mediated interactions (Spies Shapiro & Margolin, 2014). These findings have prompted a move from predominantly focusing on the influence of technology exposure among young people, to understanding the impacts (both positive and negative) of digital technologies on a range of factors concerning social and psychological development (Shapka, 2019).

One area of increasing attention is the implications of the internet for identity development, as online contexts are found to be particularly conducive for identity work in the form of exploration, self-presentation, and social interaction (Davis, 2013; Wängqvist & Frisén, 2016). However, the long-term implications of engagement with the internet during adolescence on identity has received little attention as the field of research is still relatively young, and many of the existing studies in this area are cross-sectional, or when longitudinal, focus on issues of problematic use (e.g., Anderson et al., 2017). Therefore, there is a notable lack of research investigating the implications of internet use during adolescence on identity both during this formative stage of development as well as on identity later in life. We seek to address this gap in the literature by investigating whether ease of online self-expression is associated with reduced identity integration (lower self-esteem and greater identity confusion) both concurrently during adolescence, as well as five years later in young adulthood. Furthermore, we examine the mediating effects of peer connectedness, suggesting that greater ease of self-expression online may positively influence connections with peers, and through this association, is related to increased identity integration both during adolescence and later in development.

Adolescent Identity in the Digital Era

A critical task during the formative period of adolescence is the development of a stable and authentic sense of self, or an integrated identity (Erikson, 1968). There are two major components of identity that we wish to highlight: holding beliefs and opinions about oneself that are clearly and confidently defined (identity clarity), and having a positive view of oneself, or a feeling of self-worth (self-esteem; Valkenburg & Peter, 2011; Yang & Brown, 2016). Self-expression is a central element to both self-esteem and identity clarity as it is the process through which individuals strategically communicate and control their presentation of self to others (Leary & Kowalski, 1990). With the rise of digital technologies, the internet has become an important place for adolescents to express themselves and is now considered to play a core role in the development of identity (Yang & Brown, 2016). The internet offers distinct opportunities for the construction of self through the ability to control or curate one's self-image, to safely explore facets of the self, and to encourage deeper connections with others in ways that increase self-expression (Hollenbaugh, 2021). In fact, Valkenburg and Peter (2011) argue that two important predictors of identity integration are the control over one's environment and approval and acceptance from others, both of which may be more accessible for adolescents online.

Much of the available research in this space acknowledges opportunities for easier self-expression and optimized self-presentation online. Of particular importance, the affordances of the internet, such as the ability to remain anonymous and to have greater control over how and when to respond to others (Suler, 2004), are thought to foster contexts in which self-expressions are perceived by adolescents as being easier online than face-to-face. Schouten and colleagues (2007) suggest adolescents who perceive more control over self-presentation online may feel more at ease during online self-disclosure. Additionally, Clark and Green (2018) highlight that technology-mediated interactions offer more opportunities for authentic self-presentation and identity exploration, as self-disclosure is perceived as less intimidating, more controllable, and easier in online settings.

Yet the available research exploring the impacts of online self-expression on identity development is characterized by mixed findings. Some studies have suggested adolescents are able to assert themselves more confidently online (Zhao et al., 2008) and this experience can have a lasting impact on positive perceptions of the self (Yang & Brown, 2016). In contrast, comparatively more evidence suggests engaging in online self-expression is associated with lower self-concept clarity in the form of increased identity confusion (Davis, 2013; Michikyan et al., 2015) and lower self-esteem (Meeus et al., 2019). Michikyan et al. (2015) shed further light on this association in their research finding authenticity of online self-expression was related to a more coherent sense of identity among college students. More specifically, in a recent review of the literature, it was found that inauthentic self-presentations online were consistently associated with lower self-esteem, whereas more authentic and positive self-presentations correlated with increased self-esteem (Twomey & O'Reilly, 2017). Overall, such findings suggest important associations between online self-expression and identity development and indicate the greater ease with which one engages in self-expression online may be associated with lower levels of identity clarity and self-esteem (or poorer identity integration) during adolescence. Despite the high levels of engagement with technology during adolescence and the potential for easier self-expression online (and the potential negative flow on effects for identity development), limited research has investigated how adolescents' perceptions of ease of online self-expression impact on their identity development both during adolescence and beyond.

Connection with Peers

One of the reasons for inconsistencies in the research concerning digital technology use in adolescence and identity outcomes may be that while online contexts can encourage identity exploration (and in turn, lower self-concept clarity), they also impact identity *consolidation* via increased opportunities for interaction and connection with peers (Davis, 2013). It is widely established that positive peer relationships promote identity development as they enable adolescents to learn about themselves, to explore various identity positions, and to share their sense of self with others (Meeus et al., 2002). Emerging research has found that adolescents who perceive the internet as a positive context feel safer to express themselves, are more easily able to self-disclose online, and perceive higher levels of social support, each of which have positive outcomes for identity integration (Hollenbaugh, 2021; Quinn, 2018; Schouten et al., 2007). Furthermore, a recent research review found evidence that endorsement of the internet as a means to express oneself promoted peer connectedness by increasing the accessibility of friends and enabling opportunities to actively maintain and manage relationships (Wu et al., 2016).

While there may be direct negative associations between ease of online self-expression and identity integration, online contexts also offer youth a space to connect with their peers, and in turn, foster identity clarity and self-esteem. In other words, ease of online self-expression may positively impact identity development in adolescence and into young adulthood through connections with peers. In this study we suggest that ease of online self-expression may act as a double-edged sword, whereby it is likely to be directly associated with poorer identity outcomes (increased identity confusion and decreased self-esteem), but also with increased peer connectedness which, in turn, is associated with better identity outcomes. More specifically, it is suggested that ease of self-expression in online environments may encourage peer connectedness, and in turn, promote increased identity integration.

Effects Over Time

The transition into young adulthood is an important time for young people's identity development, with previous research showing that individuals move toward a more integrated identity from adolescence into young adulthood (Kroger et al., 2010). Yet, there is a substantial gap in the research examining self-expression online in adolescence and its impact on the process of acquiring a stronger sense of integrated identity at these later stages of development. There is some short-term longitudinal evidence among young adults, with Yang and Brown (2016) finding that intentionality of expression on Facebook was related to greater reflection on the self, which in turn was associated with higher self-esteem. Furthermore, Metzler and Scheithauer (2017) found selective, positive self-expressions were associated with a higher endorsement of "likes" by peers, and in turn, lower self-esteem over time. While these studies indicate that online self-expression may have lasting effects on identity, there are still major gaps in our understanding of the impacts from adolescence to young adulthood (and beyond). One of the key reasons for the lack of research in this area is that this is a developing field, meaning there are few relevant longitudinal data sets that can shed light on these relationships. Therefore, beyond investigating the concurrent associations between online self-expression, peer connectedness, and identity development among adolescents, the current study investigated whether experiences in adolescence predicted identity integration five years later in young adulthood.

Method

Participants

The data utilized in this study form a part of the Youth Connectedness Project (YCP; Jose et al., 2012), a longitudinal study of youth in New Zealand collected annually in schools for three years between 2006 and 2008, with a follow-up online data collection five years later (2013). Adolescents aged between 9 and 16 years old were initially recruited from a wide variety of schools (e.g., mixed sex and single-sex; middle schools and high schools; religious and state schools) using a stratified random cluster sampling approach. Information sheets and consent forms were collected from adolescents and their parents within selected classes in participating schools and adolescents completed surveys via a tablet during school time. Data were collected in the same manner at time-points 1–3. At time-point 3 (in 2008), students were asked whether they would be willing to be contacted in the future and to provide several methods of contact. The follow-up survey offered five years later was matched with prior responses (Times 1–3).

The current study uses a subset of the full data, particularly focusing on youth who completed the time-point 3 (prior waves were not included due to lack of data collected about internet use). A total of 1809 young people participated in this wave and 1233 adolescents who indicated that they used the internet in their spare time were included in the current analyses (as they were asked subsequent questions about online self-expression). Therefore, the final sample was comprised of 674 females (54.5%) with an average age of 14.31 ($SD = 1.73$) at time-point 3. The majority of respondents (80.8%; $n = 999$) identified as New Zealand European, with smaller numbers identifying as Maori (Indigenous: 301: 24.4%), Pacific Islander (117: 9.3%), or identification with other ethnic groups (181: 14.7%).[1] A third (32.4%) of the sample spent an average of up to 2 hours per week chatting or surfing the internet, with 27.8% spending 3–5 hours online, 15.6% spending 6–10 hours online, and the remainder between 11 and 25 + hours per week online. The main place adolescents spent time online was BEBO (74%), a popular social networking site at the time, with other main places being MSN chat and online games.

Measures

Ease of Online Self-Expression

Perceptions of the internet as a safe and easy place for self-expression was measured with a 9-item scale developed for the purposes of this study. The prompt to the scale asked: "When communicating on the internet, is it easier or harder to do the following (compared to offline):", with example items including: "stick up for myself", "show my anger", and "not feel shy". Items were rated on a five-point scale, ranging from 1 = *Harder*, 5 = *Easier*. Higher scores on this measure indicate greater ease

---

[1] Please note that percentages are greater than 100% as adolescents were able to select more than one ethnicity in line with New Zealand standards for collecting information on ethnicity.

of self-expression in the online as compared to offline environment. The measure demonstrated high internal consistency, Cronbach's α = 0.85.

Peer Connectedness
Seven items related to peer support developed by Jose and colleagues (2012) (e.g., "*My friends and I help each other out*"), satisfaction with close friends (e.g., "*How happy are you with the amount of close friends outside school*"), and peer relations at school (e.g., "*How well do you get on with your classmates?*") were used to measure peer connectedness. All items used a five-point scale that varied across questions (Peer Support: 1 = *Strongly disagree* to 5 = *Strongly agree*; Satisfaction: 1 = *Very unhappy* to 5 = *Very happy*; Peers at School: 1 = *Not at all well* to 5 = *Really well*). The measure demonstrated adequate internal consistency, Cronbach's α = 0.78.

Identity Confusion
Three items were adapted from the Psychosocial Maturity Index (Greenberger, 1984) to measure the extent to which youth feel confusion or perceive a lack of knowledge about the self; "I don't really know what my interests are", "I change the way I feel and act so often that I sometimes wonder who the 'real' me is", and "I tend to change a lot what I like and what I don't like". These items were measured on a 5-point Likert scale ranging from 1 = *Strongly disagree* to 5 = *Strongly agree*. The Cronbach's alpha coefficients in adolescence was 0.65 and in young adulthood 0.72.

Self-Esteem
This measure was comprised of 4 items that were selected from the Rosenberg Self-Esteem Scale (Rosenberg, 1965). Participants were asked to report how much they agreed with statements such as "I feel confident and positive about myself" and "I feel that I have a number of good qualities" on a 5-point Likert scale from 1 = *Strongly disagree* to 5 = *Strongly agree*. The Cronbach's alpha coefficient for the measure in adolescence was 0.86 and in young adulthood 0.89.

Analytical Strategy

Descriptive statistics and bivariate correlations were computed in SPSS. Next, a path model was conducted in Mplus v8.2. The model combined

(1) the cross-sectional associations during adolescence concerning ease of online self-expression on identity confusion and self-esteem as mediated by peer connectedness, and (2) the longitudinal, bidirectional relationships from identity confusion and self-esteem in adolescence to the same indicators in young adulthood. The stabilities in identity outcomes over time were estimated via the inclusion of autoregressive coefficients and the effects of age, gender, and hours spent online per week were treated as covariates in the model. As a final step in the analyses, the indirect effects of adolescent measures of ease of online self-expression and peer connectedness on identity outcomes in young adulthood were examined. The significance of the indirect effects was evaluated using bootstrapped 95% confidence intervals with 5000 bootstrapped samples, with confidence intervals that do not contain zero denoting a significant indirect effect. To assess model fit we use $\chi2$, the root mean square error of approximation (RMSEA), the comparative fit index (CFI), and the standardized root mean square residual (SRMR). Good model fit is shown via the combination of these indicators, with smaller $\chi2$, RMSEA value of less than or approaching 0.06, CFI value greater than 0.95, and an SRMR value of less than 0.10 indicating good model fit. To account for missing values as a result of attrition in the longitudinal component of the model, full information maximum likelihood (FIML) was utilized.

Results

An examination of the bivariate correlations (Table 1) revealed significant, positive correlations between ease of online self-expression, peer connectedness, and identity confusion during adolescence. While self-esteem also had a positive association with peer connectedness, it was not significantly related to ease of online self-expression. Identity confusion and self-esteem were significantly negatively associated with one another within each time point as well as across time. Furthermore, peer connectedness was positively associated with self-esteem in young adulthood and negatively associated with identity confusion during young adulthood.

In the cross-sectional component of the path model, controlling for covariates, ease of online self-expression was significantly, directly, and positively associated with peer connectedness ($\beta = 0.11$, $p < 0.001$) and identity confusion ($\beta = 0.15$, $p < 0.001$) during adolescence, but it was not associated significantly with self-esteem ($\beta = 0.02$, $p > 0.05$). Additionally, peer connectedness was found to directly predict

Table 1 Descriptive statistics and correlations between indicators at adolescence and young adulthood

		1	2	3	4	5	M	SD	α
Adolescence	1. Online Self-Expression	—					3.30	0.71	0.85
	2. Peer Connectedness	0.11**	—				4.27	0.63	0.78
	3. Identity Confusion	0.14**	−0.16**	—			2.27	0.77	0.65
	4. Self-esteem	0.04	0.28**	−0.28**	—		4.07	0.68	0.86
Young Adulthood	5. Identity Confusion	0.05	−0.17**	0.32**	−0.19**	—	2.37	0.87	0.72
	6. Self-esteem	0.01	0.17**	−0.18**	0.30**	−0.34**	3.91	0.71	0.89

* $p < 0.05$, ** $p < 0.001$

identity outcomes, being significantly positively associated with self-esteem ($\beta = 0.34$, $p < 0.001$), and negatively associated with identity confusion ($\beta = -0.02$, $p < 0.001$) in adolescence. There was also a significant negative indirect effect of online self-expression through peer connectedness to identity confusion during adolescence ($\beta = -0.02$, 95%CI $= -0.04$, -0.01), alongside the direct effect ($\beta = 0.14$, $p < 0.001$, 95%CI $= 0.08$, 0.20). Furthermore, there was evidence for a weak, significant positive indirect effect of online self-expression through peer connectedness to self-esteem during adolescence ($\beta = 0.04$, 95%CI $= 0.02$, 0.05), alongside a non-significant direct effect ($\beta = 0.06$, $p = 0.06$, 95%CI $= 0.00$, 0.10).

In the longitudinal component of the model, the autoregressive coefficients were significant for both identity confusion and self-esteem from adolescence to young adulthood, but the stabilities were low. Furthermore, decreases in identity confusion were predicted by greater self-esteem over these five years. In contrast, identity confusion in adolescence did not significantly predict subsequent levels of self-esteem in young adulthood. The indirect effects over time showed that there was a significant positive indirect effect of ease of online self-expression on identity confusion during young adulthood via increased identity confusion in adolescence ($\beta = 0.05$, 95%CI $= 0.03$, 0.08). A significant positive indirect effect of peer connectedness during adolescence was also found. Specifically, peer connectedness manifested a significant, positive total indirect effect on self-esteem in young adulthood via increased self-esteem during adolescence ($\beta = 0.10$, 95%CI $= 0.07$, 0.14). Additionally, peer connectedness had a significant negative total indirect effect on identity confusion in young adulthood ($\beta = -0.13$, 95%CI $= -0.17$, -0.09) that comprised of significant indirect effects via identity confusion ($\beta = -0.095$, 95%CI $= -0.12$, -0.06) and self-esteem during adolescence ($\beta = -0.04$, 95%CI $= -0.07$, -0.01).

Discussion

Much of the research into associations between online self-expression and identity development has focused on either adolescent or young adult samples, without considering the direct and indirect longitudinal effects over time. The current study addressed this gap in the literature, finding both positive and negative effects on the development of identity in adolescence, with some evidence for persistence in these effects five years later. As expected, ease of online self-expression was concurrently associated with greater identity confusion, but also with both greater self-esteem and lower identity confusion via increased peer connectedness. Furthermore, online self-expression in adolescence was related to increases in identity confusion into young adulthood, and peer connectedness was longitudinally associated with both increased self-esteem and decreased identity confusion in young adulthood. These findings demonstrate important, long-lasting implications of developmental experiences online for one's sense of self. More specifically, we highlight that perceiving the internet to be a place that is easier to express oneself compared to in-person may have direct and lasting implications on identity confusion, but the positive and negative effects of such self-expressions are likely to be intertwined with whether or not these meet other important needs, such as building connections with peers.

Two hypotheses posed by Valkenburg and Peter (2011), namely the fragmentation and the self-concept unity hypotheses, may be particularly relevant in understanding these findings. The fragmentation hypothesis suggests that developing a coherent and clear identity may be undermined online due to the many opportunities for interactions with both friends and unknown others, and the ease with which different identities can be adopted. In line with this view, research has demonstrated an association between inauthentic self-presentation and lower self-esteem (Twomey & O'Reilly, 2017). In contrast, the self-concept unity hypothesis proposes that online environments provide adolescents with a space where they can experiment with their identity, and alongside this, have opportunities to interact with, and receive feedback from, others (Davis, 2013; Valkenburg & Peter, 2011). Applying these hypotheses more directly to our findings, we begin to better understand the protective mechanism of peer connectedness on identity integration. Specifically, ease of online self-expression was concurrently associated with greater identity confusion in adolescence, however, through peer connectedness, ease of self-expression online was associated with greater self-esteem and lower identity confusion. Furthermore, peer connectedness in adolescence had lasting effects on both increased self-esteem and decreased identity confusion in young adulthood. Therefore, our findings provide support for both the self-concept fragmentation and unity hypotheses and highlight an important role of peer connectedness in promoting identity integration.

Although our findings must be interpreted in light of the age of our data, recent research has demonstrated that the quality of daily social interactions in face-to-face, text, and social media settings is positively predictive of increased self-esteem (Subrahmanyam et al., 2020). The similar pattern of effects between the current findings and recent research demonstrates persistence of the mechanisms through which self-expressions and interactions influence self-esteem, despite considerable changes in perceptions of, approaches to, and use of the internet and social media in the last decade. The use of historical data in the current study is important and intentional as it allowed a deeper examination of the implications of online self-expression throughout adolescence into young adulthood, for people who are now adults, but were in the process of development when digital technologies started to grow in popularity. This approach is novel in the literature and allowed us to attain a nuanced understanding of how individuals' perceptions of the internet impacted their connectedness and identity development, during both adolescence and young adulthood.

The findings offer insight into the role of the internet in identity integration during adolescence and young adulthood, but there are also notable limitations. Firstly, there was a narrow focus of measures in the study, which were informed by the literature at the time. Recent research suggests that feedback, self-reflection, and authenticity may be underlying mechanisms through which online self-expressions are related to identity integration over time, and as such these should be included in future research (Metzler & Scheithauer, 2017; Yang & Brown, 2016). Further, our study focused on perceptions of ease of online self-expression, rather than examining expressive behaviors online, or even more specifically, self-expression via particular social media platforms. There are likely to be differences in the effects of true behaviors, self-reported behaviors, and attitudinal measures concerning online self-expression of identity as well as other social and psychological outcomes which need to be disentangled. Finally, the data did not allow for comprehensive tests of bidirectional effects between the constructs at regular intervals meaning that even though the results can infer associations across time, more comprehensive studies of longitudinal effects are needed. It is suggested that examining the nuanced ways that the internet is perceived and used as

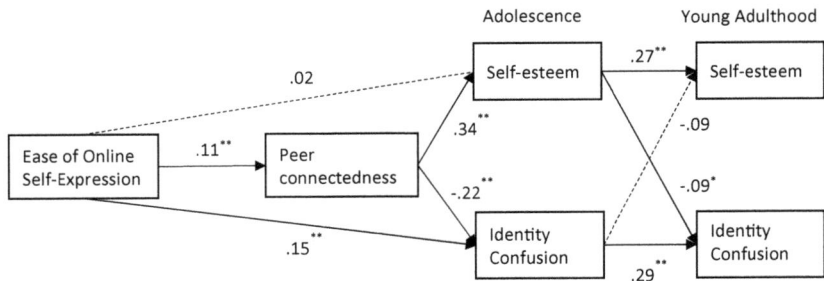

Fig. 1 Path model assessing the associations between ease of online self-expression, peer connectedness, and identity outcomes in adolescence and young adulthood (Note *p < 0.05; **p < 0.001, solid lines represent significant associations, and dashed lines non-significant associations. Model fit = χ^2 (10) = 37.80, p < 0.001; CFI = 0.96; SRMR = 0.04; RMSEA = 0.05; 95%CI = 0.03, 0.06)

a tool of self-expression should be a focus of future long-term longitudinal research.

Our experiences, and the contexts in which they occur—particularly during adolescence—shape who we are, how we see ourselves, and where we belong in society. In the current study, we demonstrated that online environments (in a time when they were gaining popularity), helped to shape young people's identity development. It has recently been suggested that the concept of the "digital native" is losing relevance due to the increasing exposure to technology across the life span (Evans & Robertson, 2020). Yet little research has sought to examine how growing up with the internet in everyday life may have impacted the identity processes of those who were once considered natives of the digital world due to being surrounded by, embedded in, and connected to many forms of internet-connected technologies throughout their formative years. This study has made an important step toward illuminating the lasting implications of online contexts on identity development, and the importance of peer connections to these identity processes. We suggest that for the purposes of growing the field of cyberpsychology, it may be the case that we need to look backwards before we can move forwards in order to truly understand the long-term impacts of the internet on identity (Fig. 1).

References

Anderson, E. L., Steen, E., & Stavropoulos, V. (2017). Internet use and problematic internet use: A systematic review of longitudinal research trends in adolescence and emergent adulthood. *International Journal of Adolescence and Youth, 22*(4), 430–454. https://doi.org/10.1080/02673843.2016.1227716

Clark, J. L., & Green, M. C. (2018). The social consequences of online interaction. In A. Attrill-Smith, C. Fullwood, M. Keep., & D. J. Kuss (Eds.), *The Oxford handbook of cyberpsychology*. Oxford University Press. https://doi.org/10.1093/oxfordhb/9780198812746.013.14

Davis, K. (2013). Young people's digital lives: The impact of interpersonal relationships and digital media use on adolescents' sense of identity. *Computers in Human Behavior, 29*(6), 2281–2293. https://doi.org/10.1016/j.chb.2013.05.022

Erikson, E.H. (1968). *Identity: Youth and crisis*. Norton & Co.

Evans, C., & Robertson, W. (2020). The four phases of the digital natives debate. *Human Behavior and Emerging Technologies, 2*(3), 269–277. https://doi.org/10.1002/hbe2.196

Greenberger, E. (1984). Defining psychosocial maturity in adolescence. *Advances in Child Behavioral Analysis & Therapy, 3*, 1–37.

Helsper, E. J., & Eynon, R. (2010). Digital natives: Where is the evidence? *British Educational Research Journal, 36*(3), 503–520. https://doi.org/10.1080/01411920902989227

Hollenbaugh, E. E. (2021). Self-presentation in social media: Review and research opportunities. *Review of Communication Research, 9*, 80–98. https://doi.org/10.12840/ISSN.2255-4165.027

Jose, P. E., Ryan, N., & Pryor, J. (2012). Does social connectedness promote a greater sense of well-being in adolescence over time? *Journal of Research on Adolescence, 22*(2), 235–251. https://doi.org/10.1111/j.1532-7795.2012.00783.x

Kroger, J., Martinussen, M., & Marcia, J. E. (2010). Identity status change during adolescence and young adulthood: A meta-analysis. *Journal of Adolescence, 33*(5), 683–698. https://doi.org/10.1016/j.adolescence.2009.11.002

Leary, M. R., & Kowalski, R. M. (1990). Impression management: A literature review and two-component model. *Psychological Bulletin, 107*(1), 34. https://doi.org/10.1037/0033-2909.107.1.34

Meeus, A., Beullens, K., & Eggermont, S. (2019). Like me (please?): Connecting online self-presentation to pre- and early adolescents' self-esteem. *New Media & Society, 21*(11–12), 2386–2403. https://doi.org/10.1177/1461444819847447

Meeus, W. I. M., Oosterwegel, A., & Vollebergh, W. (2002). Parental and peer attachment and identity development in adolescence. *Journal of Adolescence*, 25(1), 93–106. https://doi.org/10.1006/jado.2001.0451

Metzler, A., & Scheithauer, H. (2017). The long-term benefits of positive self-presentation via profile pictures, number of friends and the initiation of relationships on Facebook for adolescents' self-esteem and the initiation of offline relationships. *Frontiers in Psychology*, 8, 1981. https://doi.org/10.3389/fpsyg.2017.01981

Michikyan, M., Dennis, J., & Subrahmanyam, K. (2015). Can you guess who I am? Real, ideal, and false self-presentation on Facebook among emerging adults. *Emerging Adulthood*, 3(1), 55–64. https://doi.org/10.1177/2167696814532442

Prenksy, M. (2001). Digital natives, digital immigrants. *On the Horizon*, 9(5), 1–6.

Quinn, S. (2018). Positive aspects of social media. In A. Attrill-Smith, C. Fullwood, M. Keep., & D. J. Kuss (Eds.) *The Oxford handbook of cyberpsychology*. Oxford University Press. https://doi.org/10.1093/oxfordhb/9780198812746.013.23

Rosenberg, M. (1965). *Society and the adolescent self-image*. Princeton University Press.

Schouten, A. P., Valkenburg, P. M., & Peter, J. (2007). Precursors and underlying processes of adolescents' online self-disclosure: Developing and testing an "Internet-attribute-perception" model. *Media Psychology*, 10, 292–315. https://doi.org/10.1080/15213260701375686

Shapka, J. D. (2019). Adolescent technology engagement: It is more complicated than a lack of self-control. *Human Behavior and Emerging Technologies*, 1(2), 103–110. https://doi.org/10.1002/hbe2.144

Spies Shapiro, L. A. S., & Margolin, G. (2014). Growing up wired: Social networking sites and adolescent psychosocial development. *Clinical Child and Family Psychology Review*, 17(1), 1–18. https://doi.org/10.1007/s10567-013-0135-1

Suler, J. (2004). The online disinhibition effect. *Cyberpsychology & Behavior*, 7, 321–326. https://doi.org/10.1089/1094931041291295

Subrahmanyam, K., Frison, E., & Michikyan, M. (2020). The relation between face-to-face and digital interactions and self-esteem: A daily diary study. *Human Behavior and Emerging Technologies*, 2(2), 116–127. https://doi.org/10.1002/hbe2.187

Twomey, C., & O'Reilly, G. (2017). Associations of self-presentation on Facebook with mental health and personality variables: A systematic review. *Cyberpsychology, Behavior and Social Networking*, 20(10), 587–595. https://doi.org/10.1089/cyber.2017.0247

Valkenburg, P. M., & Peter, J. (2011). Online communication among adolescents: An integrated model of its attraction, opportunities, and risks. *Journal of Adolescent Health, 48,* 121–127. https://doi.org/10.1016/j.jadohealth.2010.08.020

Wängqvist, M., & Frisén, A. (2016). Who am I online? Understanding the meaning of online contexts for identity development. *Adolescent Research Review, 1*(2), 139–151. https://doi.org/10.1007/s40894-016-0025-0

Wu, Y. J., Outley, C., Matarrita-Cascante, D., & Murphrey, T. P. (2016). A systematic review of recent research on adolescent social connectedness and mental health with internet technology use. *Adolescent Research Review, 1*(2), 153–162. https://doi.org/10.1007/s40894-015-0013-9

Yang, C. C., & Brown, B. B. (2016). Online self-presentation on Facebook and self development during the college transition. *Journal of Youth and Adolescence, 45*(2), 402–416. https://doi.org/10.1007/s10964-015-0385-y

Zhao, S., Grasmuck, S., & Martin, J. (2008). Identity construction on Facebook: Digital empowerment in anchored relationships. *Computers in Human Behavior, 24*(5), 1816–1836. https://doi.org/10.1016/j.chb.2008.02.012

Communication, Social Support, and Families

Susan Abel and John Gilmour

Abstract Social support can facilitate better mental and physical health and buffer individuals in times of stress. Social media sites like Facebook provide individuals with an additional avenue to access social support. Online interaction also complements face-to-face communication for intergenerational family engagement. This chapter explores how social support operates online and discusses the ways in which social media has seeped into the fabric of family interactions for humans across the lifespan. While there are obstacles posed by online interaction, digital media practices can help overcome time and distance barriers for many families and provide connection across the lifespan.

Keywords Social media · Social support · Communication · Families · Kinkeeping

---

S. Abel
University of Southern Queensland, Toowoomba, QLD, Australia

J. Gilmour (✉)
The University of Queensland, Brisbane, QLD, Australia
e-mail: john.stephen.gilmour@gmail.com

© The Author(s), under exclusive license to Springer Nature Switzerland AG 2022
T. Machin et al. (eds.), *Social Media and Technology Across the Lifespan*, Palgrave Studies in Cyberpsychology,
https://doi.org/10.1007/978-3-030-99049-7_5

Introduction

This chapter explores how social media can be a source of support, connection, and conflict for families across the lifespan. The chapter draws on research conducted with 43 social media users as part of two more extensive studies. The first study investigated social support provided via Facebook through semi-structured interviews with 15 social media users from regional areas in south-eastern Queensland and northern New South Wales, Australia, in 2016. All participants had to be over 18 years old and have an active social media account accessed at least weekly. The interview questions were focused on social media use, methods of social engagement on Facebook, and family and local community engagement via Facebook. The second study investigated family communication using social media in 2020 through semi-structured interviews with 28 social media users across Australia. Interview questions focused on the types of social media individuals used with family, their motivations for doing so, and issues around privacy and availability online. Participant quotes and an image from these studies illuminate ideas within this chapter by providing explicit examples and providing the reader with context for the importance of social media at many stages in life (Lingard, 2019). The chapter provides an exploration of social media use for support or family practices in five contexts: early and middle childhood, adolescents, young adults, at midlife, and older adults.

Families use a wide array of social media for their online activities, from private channels like WhatsApp to the collapsed context of Facebook (see Abel et al., 2021). The channels used by individuals to "do family" vary in accordance with their levels of digital literacy, access to affordable technology, and the distance between them and their contacts. When we think of *distance*, we imagine geography, but temporal distance is also a factor. For families separated indefinitely, video calls are a critical element of their family practices (Abel et al., 2021). For those who live in the same country and have opportunities to see each other more frequently, video calls seem to be limited to grandparent-grandchild communication or family rituals such as weddings (Share et al., 2017). All families engage in rituals to create their family identity and maintain relationships (see Wolin & Bennett, 1984). When there is no imminent possibility of face-to-face contact, people adapt patterned routines using social media to foster ambient co-presence. These routines can be as simple as a daily wakeup call, or an absent parent assisting with their child's homework (Brown, 2016).

Social media could be seen as only offering an extension of traditional forms of mediated communication such as the telephone or letter. However, this chapter contends that the ubiquity of the mobile phone and its affordance of portability has fundamentally changed the way families communicate (Schrock, 2015). The potential for almost permanent connectivity and an ambient awareness of each other's lives means that this current generation of families could know more about their parents and offspring than any other.

Social media can be used as a means to access social networks that can provide support to individuals. Social support is considered to be crucial for human health and wellbeing (Cohen & Wills, 1985; Taylor, 2011). Social support has been found to buffer a person from the adverse physical and psychological effects of stress and provide greater feelings of wellbeing and life satisfaction (Cohen & Wills, 1985; Taylor, 2011; Zhang, 2017). Using social media as a mechanism for social support has been associated with better mental and physical health (Kim & Lee, 2011; Nabi et al., 2013). Studies have found that higher levels of social media-based social support (i.e., social support drawn from online interactions) can predict lower levels of perceived stress, physical illness, and mental distress, as well as increase the likelihood of a person seeking out health services (Frison & Eggermont, 2015; Kim & Lee, 2011; Nabi et al., 2013; Wright et al., 2013). Online social support has been found to assist individuals with limited social opportunities or little inclination to seek support in a face-to-face context (Indian & Grieve, 2014; Miller, 2008). It is also worth noting that currently, young adults and adolescents appear to utilise social media as means of social support when compared to older adults (65 years and older; Chan, 2018).

SOCIAL MEDIA USE STARTS IN EARLY CHILDHOOD

Social media has become fully integrated into modern social life, with many children being introduced to social media during key childhood developmental stages. Children, like many adults, view social media as an opportunity to make new friends, communicate with existing friends, and play social media-based games (Hadjipanayis et al., 2019). Unlike many adults, children do not fully understand the risks associated with social media use, such as online predation, bullying, and social media overuse (Richards et al., 2015; Tartari, 2015).

Generally, children two years of age and younger require hands-on activities and interactions with parents or caregivers to develop socially (Hadjipanayis et al., 2019). Because of this, toddlers will generally not benefit from interacting with digital media as much as they would with in-person interactions. However, as many parents utilise video calls as a way for toddlers to engage with inaccessible relatives, it is worth noting that using video calls can be beneficial in building relationships if parents engage with toddlers to help them understand the context of the social interaction (Hadjipanayis et al., 2019).

Social media interaction for preschool-aged children is also not ideal for social and cognitive development, as young children tend to benefit from unstructured social play and parent–child interactions (Hadjipanayis et al., 2019). An additional concern for parents is that their excessive use of mobile devices can impact their child's development and increase parent–child conflict (Hadjipanayis et al., 2019). Generally, 13 years old is the minimum age requirement for most well-known social media sites. However, this has led to a rise in falsified profiles (Fernández, 2011; Ho et al., 2017). It is estimated that nearly 40% of the self-reported 13–19-year-old population of Facebook is actually below this age limit (Fernández, 2011; Ho et al., 2017). This suggests that children are engaging with social media at a much younger age than the limits the sites themselves have set. It is also worth noting that the false identity created for social media (sometimes called the "Facebook Self") is especially seductive to children in order to be accepted and praised by their peer group (Fernández, 2011; Ho et al., 2017). Children's falsification of social media profiles also allows them access to content, and a means to express themselves, which parents and caregivers would typically not allow. Additionally, children may spend large amounts of time on social media, leading to reduced sleep time and poor quality sleep (Swist et al., 2015).

There are several positives associated with social media use and children Social media is now playing a significant role in socialising children, and children without social media can face social exclusion (Swist et al., 2015). Most children use social media to communicate with their existing social circle, making it crucial for social development and inclusion. It is worth noting that parents of children will make use of social media to organise time with other parents for their children to play and spend time together and use social media to link in with activities for their children. As Stacey (aged 34), an interviewee living in Australia, notes:

> However, mostly I'm on [social media] just to see what is happening around us if I want to take the kids to something....I also keep it because it's just a really good way of getting to know who my kids' friends' parents are....it's not only our interests [on social media] that we have, it's the kids' interests as well. (Stacey)

Once children reach adolescence, social media has become a key component of adolescent communication and social development. Many adolescents consider social media is essential to building and maintaining social ties (Anderson & Jiang, 2018; Tartari, 2015).

Adolescent Social Media Use Support, Bullying, and Family Interaction

Most adolescents in developed countries use some form of social media, with approximately 85% using multiple platforms (e.g., Instagram, TikTok, Facebook; Anderson & Jiang, 2018). It has been found that the use of social media by adolescents is considered a cost-effective form of communication. As social media sites, like Facebook and Instagram, use on mobile platforms can be included as free in many mobile plans, adolescents have been utilising social media to engage with social networks rather than traditional calls or testing. Gaile described having many younger friends who could not afford a full plan and use social media, in this case, Facebook, to maintain contact:

> I have some young friends who are too poor to keep their phones working, so Facebook, it's just a bit of data. So we message through Messenger, where it's just data rather than a call. (Gaile)

However, while many adolescents use social media as a mechanism to build and maintain supportive networks, many pitfalls can cause significant distress or harm to younger users. Cyberbullying on social media is a concern for adolescents, with 27% of teens reporting being bullied online (Anderson & Jiang, 2018). Additionally, exposure to adult or distressing materials can cause issues with mental health. The use of social media to send images or videos that are sexual in nature is also a concern for adolescent users (Richards et al., 2015; Tartari, 2015). However, all social media use is not inherently harmful.

Social media can provide adolescents with a digital medium for social supportMany adolescents will seek support from peers via social media rather than face-to-face, positively affecting mental health (Frison & Eggermont, 2015; Gilmour et al., 2020). Many adolescents are more comfortable with communicating emotional content via mediums like Facebook rather than in person. Additionally, female adolescents are more likely to feel supported by social media than males (Frison & Eggermont, 2016; Gilmour et al., 2020). It is worth noting that adolescents supporting victimised peers will often feel victimised themselves, which can negatively impact their wellbeing (Cole et al., 2017; Gilmour et al., 2020).

While adolescents may spurn the family group chat as hard as their parents attempt to engage with them (Aharony & Gazit, 2016), social media comes into its own when they depart the family home, and intergenerational contact occurs at a distance. Parents have long provided social and instrumental support through mediated communication to their emerging adult children (e.g., Rakow & Navarro, 1993). However, new technologies such as mobile social media may contribute to closer emotional ties by facilitating co-presence and a sense of satisfactory care at a distance (Baldassar, 2016).

Young Adults Maintaining Family Connections at a Distance

Young adults, or persons aged 18–30 years, are considered very active on social media, with 69% reporting using multiple social media sites multiple times a day (Anderson et al., 2021). The use of social media has become a key component in young adults' ability to connect and remain connected with friends and family (Gilmour et al., 2019; Indian & Grieve, 2014). Many young adults have to relocate for work, which can be isolating (Bates, 2014). They use social media and video chat-based communication to remain in contact with family members and maintain social ties with friends. In her early 20s, Sandra describes moving to a regional area and how social media has helped maintain social ties.

> Well, I think [social media] is huge in being able to keep in contact with all my friends that live out of town. Because I lived in [another city] for about seven years, so I do have a lot of friends up there. (Sandra)

Social media has become so interconnected in modern-day social life that many online communities have been developed to foster and maintain what would have previously been in-person social networks (Gilmour et al., 2019; Indian & Grieve, 2014). Many social media users have developed online communities specific to their local area and utilise them for professional and personal reasons. Margret, a 22-year-old journalist, describes using social media to stay in contact with friends and for work:

> I use [social media] quite a bit for work. I moved interstate at the end of last year, so I use it quite a lot to keep in touch with friends too…. [I] like community groups; and those kind of local area [groups]. I was a part of quite a few groups when I was in high school and I think those groups are still existent but they're not active anymore, if you know what I mean. (Margret)

Beyond this, young adults' non-use of social media can lead to the fear of missing out on key social interactions and events. This can lead to many young adults feeling like they must have at least one social media account to stay current in their social circles (Anderson et al., 2021; Reer et al., 2019). Young adults overwhelmingly accept their parents as Facebook friends and believe parental posts about them are tokens of care (Yang, 2018). However, this also impacts young adults' self-presentation as they often curate their content, so it is acceptable for parental viewing. One method young adults like Emma use to mitigate against this self-censorship is to create alternate profiles so they can curate their audience:

> We call them spam Instagrams. Where you just post like stupid stuff that you don't need the world to see. It's for your close friends kind of. Like if something funny has happened at work or you've had a funny text, like chat with somebody, and you post it. (Emma)

It is not only younger people who have adopted social media as a connection and social support mechanism. Almost three-quarters of American adults report using social media are middle-aged (50–64 years), and about half the population of older adults are social media users (Auxier & Anderson, 2021).

Roles and Responsibilities Online at Mid-Life

Individual mid-life experiences vary widely on every issue of interest to scholars, such as health, marital status, the existence of children or grandchildren. One aspect middle-aged adults have in common is that they have more living family members than younger or older adults (Fingerman & Birditt, 2003). Middle-aged adults are also more interested in engaging with this multiplicity of family members—adult children, grandchildren, siblings, and parents (Fingerman et al., 2004). Given the high mobility among this age group, social media offers a platform for middle-aged adults to engage with families living across distributed households and perform their family roles and care responsibilities (Matassi et al., 2019; Wulff et al., 2010).

Family experiences of social media are not always positive and sometimes involve conflict. Some middle-aged parents find that social media use causes friction with their young adult children due to parental perceptions that it is intrusive on family time (Barrie et al., 2019). In turn, children can sometimes find their parents' behaviour intrusive when they perceive parental online comments are inappropriate or the parent engages in offline conversations about the child's posts (Barrie et al., 2019). The types of "mistakes" parents make in the context of Facebook etiquette transgressing actions such as: posting private messages on the relative's wall instead of sending a private message, using inappropriate emojis (e.g., the crying with laughter emoji instead of the sad emoji) or making overly personal or protective comments on relative's posts that their friends can see. Amanda's experience on Facebook is typical when she says her mother:

> Doesn't really know how to use Facebook, so it's a bit cringeworthy. If I've put a comment on someone's post, and then she should come back and reply to my comment. No! She doesn't! She just replies to the whole thread! So that I'm sure people are like, 'Oh my god, who is this woman?' She'll say a comment and then she'll do a heart, which is fine, and then a weird emoji face. (Amanda)

In contrast, some middle-aged parents believed seeing their children's social media posts and engaging in the family group chat has resulted in them feeling more closely connected with their children's lives than their parents experienced. As Tiffany (53 years) says about her young adult daughter:

Rachel's a bigger user on, probably on Facebook and Instagram and certainly when she was living away from us, we would have a much better idea of what's going on in her life. Yeah, Mum, my mum wouldn't have known a thing. (Tiffany)

Being connected and staying connected online often requires someone in the family, known as a kinkeeper, who is more motivated than others to maintain family bonds (Rosenthal, 1985). Kinkeeping using social media is a gendered role, typically held by a middle-aged woman. The role involves using mediated technology to maintain contact with other family members, encouraging them to interact, organising family events, encouraging member participation in these rituals, and facilitating caregiving within the family (Braithwaite et al., 2017; Shaker, 2018). Ruby (aged 19) identifies her middle-aged mother's social media kinkeeping role when talking about who does the most family connection work:

She shares stuff that we might all be interested in, and she likes all of our posts on Facebook. She comments. She reminds us about birthdays. She organises trips so I can come see the family. She organises trips so my brothers can see me. (Ruby)

OLDER ADULTS: "GREY DIGITAL DIVIDE" OR SELECTIVE USE?

Grandparents learn to use Skype or Facebook Messenger—often with the support of their adult children—to video-chat with their very young grandchildren to build authentic relationships (Nedelcu, 2017). They often continue to follow older grandchildren on Facebook to keep in touch with their daily lives (Ivan & Hebblethwaite, 2016). Of course, it is not only intergenerational connections that are supported by social media. Sibling friendships, where they exist, are one of the longest-lasting relationships people maintain in their lifetime (Dunn, 2014). Older adult siblings frequently utilise the collapsed context of Facebook and private channels such as group chats to share their interests and provide social support (e.g., Cabalquinto, 2018).

Age-related factors are frequently implicated as barriers to older adult engagement with social media (Mubarak & Nycyk, 2017). While it is acknowledged that older people's use of social media is increasing (Anderson & Perrin, 2017), the "grey digital divide": is often conceptualised as an issue of limited digital literacy whereby older peoples' social media use is constrained by their lack of confidence to access and use technology (e.g., Bell et al., 2013). However, in reality, this group of technology users is highly diverse in their motivations for use, online activity, digital literacy, and prior technology experiences (Jokisch et al., 2020; van Boekel et al., 2017). The digital divide between those who have access to technology and understand how to use it and those who are locked out—is less related to chronological age than existing inequalities in society such as income, education, migration status, and living in an urban vs. rural location (Haight et al., 2014). One of the ways age intersects with disadvantage is that individuals can be displaced into populations with few resources as they age. For example, retirement may lead to a person entering a lower income group and thus have fewer resources to allocate to technology (Hargittai & Dobransky, 2017). Older adults from more privileged backgrounds with higher socioeconomic status and educational levels are more likely to be digitally literate and are better able to access technology as they age (Hargittai et al., 2019).

Technology adoption factors relevant to this chapter that positively influence older adults to use social media include social support, technical support, and motivation (Lee & Coughlin, 2015). Family descendants can play a vital role in all three factors. People with supportive family members who encourage them to adopt technology and engage with them on social media are more able to overcome previous digital illiteracy (e.g., Mead & Neves, 2018). While some older adults rate their digital literacy as inadequate compared to younger relatives, they also demonstrate confidence in their abilities to work out how to use technology (Quan-Haase et al., 2018). For example, Linda is 69 years old and lives alone in regional Queensland. She regularly engages in lively discussions with her four adult children using WhatsApp, Instagram, and Facebook and values social media as a means of frequently seeing images of her grandchildren. Linda lacks confidence in her digital skills and is reluctant to ask for technical help from her children. Despite these barriers, she is highly motivated to connect and displays tenaciousness in learning to access the technology she needs:

> The things that I don't know about I mostly can work out on my own and if I can't get through it I just give up and only do the things I can do. I wouldn't dream of taking any time from anyone. The way I figure it is, I'm not really important and if I can't work it out, it's my fault and I'd better find out a way to work it out…I didn't have my mother saying,

'Linda come and help me with blah, blah'. She got on with it! So, I just have to be smarter, or be more persistent, or find a different way. You can get some IT problems solved by paying $25 for a session at an iLove Computers shop you know. I think there are a lot of old people who are very capable. They've risen to the challenge...and on their phones they've got their daughters and they share pictures, and they text, and they've got a laptop that they look at realestate.com on. So, they can do things that they want to do that are important for them, but they wouldn't go past that, they've got no need to. (Linda)

Maintaining these family bonds are particularly important to older adults as shrinking connections (loss of peers and family members) become a challenge to their wellbeing (Wherton et al., 2015). Social support gained through close relationships with kin, particularly those with siblings, children, and grandchildren, becomes increasingly important as people age (Segrin & Flora, 2018). Keeping in touch with family members is a crucial motivator to use social media for most older adults (Zickuhr & Madden, 2012). In turn, social media adoption can lead to improved wellbeing. Older adults who adopt social media report higher perceived social support (Yu et al., 2015). Social support via social media may have broader implications for mental health in an older cohort. Adoption of social media is related to reduced depression, decreased loneliness, and better life satisfaction (Hunsaker & Hargittai, 2018).

Daniel, a 63-year-old, retired Facebook user, discussed using social media to stay in contact with family and pursue interests following his wife's death:

For checking things out, people, keeping in contact with relatives, friends, just investigating things. I like – I'm a bit of a history nut, so I like things like Time Team and archaeology and Australian coins. Most of my family's spread all around Australia, and the world actually, so we use [social media]. We Skype every [week], with my son and grandsons. (Daniel)

Older adults also report being proxy users who demonstrate care by sharing social media content with their older relatives who are unable to use the technology (Taipale, 2019). For example, Diane, aged 67 expresses care for her 90-year-old mother during her weekly visits by showing her the images and stories Diane has screenshot from her Facebook feed:

> So what I do, I get all the photos here and I take my iPad around and go through and show her the photos I've got through, through Facebook or through Messenger. It's of interest to her because she's outside the media if you'd like to put it that way. It just gives her something else to think about and to see, and it changes her day. (Diane)

While differences in digital accessand use remain across socioeconomic lines (Hartnett, 2017), participants like Diane found the affordability and accessibility of social media led to more frequent communication, open disclosure, and closer bonds with their children compared to their own youthful experiences when telephone calls were costly:

> You didn't talk to your mother about those different things. Whereas I find kids these days are more open because you have a chain of communication these days. I wouldn't even speak to Mum much when I was working because I lived with Nanna and Pop. It was only by phone and I had to pay for the phone call. We were on very low wage and we didn't have mobile service. So I wouldn't probably speak to Mum unless I went home for the weekend. Yeah, so it's totally different. (Diane)

By this point, social media has become a staple for many older adults though not always in the way younger users have adopted it. The use of social media has become so commonplace that it is difficult to imagine modern times without access to social networking sites.

Overall, families are using social media in various ways to support each other and maintain their bonds. The mitigation measures taken in the West against the spread of COVID-19, such as lockdowns and border closures, have meant social media can play a crucial role. Indeed, during COVID-19 lockdowns, some older adults were so motivated to combat the social isolation that they overcame reluctance to use platforms such as Facebook Messenger to share photos and content with friends and family. One such user, Bev, enjoyed the feeling of community by marking birthdays in a group chat by sharing images of typical celebration meals such as cake and wine (see Fig. 1).

In summary, families will continue to find novel ways of maintaining bonds and providing social support online between and within the generations. While social scientists continue to frame research around the dysfunctional consequences of social media use (Kapoor et al., 2018), perhaps it is time to stop viewing social media through the perspective of modernisation vs. traditionalism which considers social media a threat

Fig. 1 Bev's birthday message (*Source* Personal communication, Bev. Used with permission)

to cultural and moral values (Enli & Skogerbø, 2013). Perhaps it is time that like Bev, social science researchers overcome their fears of new media technology to focus on how people on either side of the screen support each other and deepen their bonds.

References

Abel, S., Machin, T., & Brownlow, C. (2021). Social media, rituals, and long-distance family relationship maintenance: A mixed-methods systematic review. *New Media & Society, 23*(3), 632–654. https://doi.org/10.1177/1461444820958717

Aharony, N., & Gazit, T. (2016). The importance of the Whatsapp family group: An exploratory analysis. *Aslib Journal of Information Management, 68*(2), 174–192. https://doi.org/10.1108/AJIM-09-2015-0142

Anderson, M., & Jiang, J. (2018, May 31). *Teens, social media & technology 2018*. Pew Research Center. Retrieved April 20, 2021, from https://www.pewresearch.org/internet/2018/05/31/teens-social-media-technology-2018/

Anderson, M., & Perrin, A. (2017, May 17). *Tech adoption climbs among older Americans*. Pew Research Center. Retrieved April 20,

2021, from https://www.pewresearch.org/internet/2017/05/17/tech-ado ption-climbs-among-older-adults/

Anderson, M., Rainie, L., & Nolan, H. (2021, April 7). *Social Media Use in 2021* Pew Research Centre. Retrieved April 20, 2021, from https://www. pewresearch.org/internet/2021/04/07/social-media-use-in-2021/

Baldassar, L. (2016). De-demonizing distance in mobile family lives: Co-presence, care circulation and polymedia as vibrant matter. *Global Networks, 16*(2), 145–163. https://doi.org/10.1111/glob.12109

Barrie, C. K., Bartkowski, J. P., & Haverda, T. (2019). The digital divide among parents and their emerging adult children: Intergenerational accounts of technologically assisted family communication. *Social Sciences, 8*(3), 83. https://doi.org/10.3390/socsci8030083

Bates, T. K. (2014). Relocation to an area of high amenity: Tree-change euphoria vs. homesickness, alienation and loneliness. *Australian Community Psychologist, 26*(1). Retrieved January 24, 2020, fromhttps://www.academia. edu/8404888/Relocation_to_an_area_of_high_amenity_Tree-change_eup horia_vs._homesickness_alienation_and_loneliness

Bell, C., Fausset, C., Farmer, S., Nguyen, J., Harley, L., & Fain, W. B. (2013). Examining social media use among older adults. *Proceedings of the 24th ACM Conference on Hypertext and Social Media,* 158–163. https://doi.org/10. 1145/2481492.2481509

Braithwaite, D. O., Marsh, J. S., Tschampl-Diesing, C. L., et al. (2017). "Love Needs to Be Exchanged": A diary study of interaction and enactment of the family kinkeeper role. *Western Journal of Communication, 81*(5), 601–618. https://doi.org/10.1080/10570314.2017.1299881

Brown, R. H. (2016). Multiple modes of care: Internet and the formation of care networks in Israel. *Global Networks, 16*(2016), 237–256. https://doi. org/10.1111/glob.12112

Cabalquinto, E. C. (2018). Home on the move: Negotiating differential domesticity in family life at a distance. *Media Culture & Society, 40*(6), 795–816. https://doi.org/10.1177/0163443717737611

Chan, M. (2018). Mobile-mediated multimodal communications, relationship quality and subjective wellbeing: An analysis of smartphone use from a life course perspective. *Computers in Human Behavior, 87,* 254–262. https:// doi.org/10.1016/j.chb.2018.05.027

Cohen, S., & Wills, T. A. (1985). Stress, social support, and the buffering hypothesis. *Psychological Bulletin, 98*(2), 310. https://doi.org/10.1037// 0033-2909.98.2.310

Cole, D. A., Nick, E. A., Zelkowitz, R. L., Roeder, K. M., & Spinelli, T. (2017). Online social support for young people: Does it recapitulate in-person social support; can it help? *Computers in Human Behavior, 68,* 456–464. https:// doi.org/10.1016/j.chb.2016.11.058

Dunn, J. (2014). Sibling relationships across the life-span. In S. Sherwin-White, and D. Hindle (Eds.), *Sibling matters: A psychoanalytic, developmental, and systemic approach* (1st ed., pp. 69–81). Routledge.

Enli, G. S., & Skogerbø, E. (2013). Personalized campaigns in party-centred politics. *Information Communication & Society, 16*(5), 757–774. https://doi.org/10.1080/1369118X.2013.782330

Fernández, A. (2011). Clinical Report: The impact of social media on children, adolescents and families. *Archivos de Pediatría del Uruguay, 82*(1), 31–32. Retrieved April 20, 2021, from http://pediatrics.aappublications.org/cgi/content/full/127/4/800?

Fingerman, K. L., & Birditt, K. S. (2003). Do age differences in close and problematic family ties reflect the pool of available relatives? *The Journals of Gerontology Series B: Psychological Sciences and Social Sciences, 58*(2), 80–87. https://doi.org/10.1093/geronb/58.2.P80

Fingerman, K. L., Nussbaum, J., & Birditt, K. S. (2004). Keeping all five balls in the air: Juggling family communication at midlife. In A. L. Vangelisti (Ed.), *Handbook of family communication* (pp. 135–152). Lawrence Erlbaum Associates Publishers.

Frison, E., & Eggermont, S. (2015). The impact of daily stress on adolescents' depressed mood: The role of social support seeking through Facebook. *Computers in Human Behavior, 44*, 315–325. https://doi.org/10.1016/j.chb.2014.11.070

Frison, E., & Eggermont, S. (2016). Exploring the relationships between different types of Facebook use, perceived online social support, and adolescents' depressed mood. *Social Science Computer Review, 34*(2), 153–171. https://doi.org/10.1177/0894439314567449

Gilmour, J., Machin, T., Brownlow, C., & Jeffries, C. (2019). Facebook-based social support and health: A systematic review. *Psychology of Popular Media Culture.* https://doi.org/10.1037/ppm0000246

Gilmour, J., Machin, T., Brownlow, C., & Jeffries, C. (2020). Facebook-based social support and health: A systematic review. *Psychology of Popular Media, 9*(3), 328–346. https://doi.org/10.1037/ppm0000246

Hadjipanayis, A., Efstathiou, E., Altorjai, P., Stiris, T., Valiulis, A., Koletzko, B., & Fonseca, H. (2019). Social media and children: What is the paediatrician's paediatrician's role? *European Journal of Pediatrics, 178*(10), 1605–1612. https://doi.org/10.1007/s00431-019-03458-w

Haight, M., Quan-Haase, A., & Corbett, B. A. (2014). Revisiting the digital divide in Canada: The impact of demographic factors on access to the internet, level of online activity, and social networking site usage. *Information Communication and Society, 17*(4), 503–519. https://doi.org/10.1080/1369118X.2014.891633

Hargittai, E., & Dobransky, K. (2017). Old dogs, new clicks: Digital inequality in skills and uses among older adults. *Canadian Journal of Communication, 42*(2), 195–212. https://doi.org/10.22230/cjc.2017v42n2a3176

Hargittai, E., Piper, A. M., & Morris, M. R. (2019). From internet access to internet skills: Digital inequality among older adults. *Universal Access in the Information Society, 18*(4), 881–890. https://doi.org/10.1007/s10209-018-0617-5

Hartnett, M. (2017). Differences in the digital home lives of young people in New Zealand. *British Journal of Educational Technology, 48*(2), 642–652. https://doi.org/10.1111/bjet.12430

Ho, S. S., Chen, L., & Ng, A. P. (2017). Comparing cyberbullying perpetration on social media between primary and secondary school students. *Computers & Education, 109*, 74–84. https://doi.org/10.1016/j.compedu.2017.02.004

Hunsaker, A., & Hargittai, E. (2018). A review of Internet use among older adults. *New Media and Society, 20*(10), 3937–3954. https://doi.org/10.1177/1461444818787348

Indian, M., & Grieve, R. (2014, Mar). When Facebook is easier than face-to-face: Social support derived from Facebook in socially anxious individuals. *Personality and individual differences, 59*, 102–106. https://doi.org/10.1016/j.paid.2013.11.016

Ivan, L., & Hebblethwaite, S. (2016). Grannies on the net: Grandmothers' experiences of Facebook in family communication. *Romanian Journal of Communication and Public Relations, 18*(1), 11–25. https://doi.org/10.21018/rjcpr.2016.1.199

Jokisch, M. R., Schmidt, L. I., Doh, M., Marquard, M., & Wahl, H.-W. (2020). The role of internet self-efficacy, innovativeness and technology avoidance in breadth of internet use: Comparing older technology experts and non-experts. *Computers in Human Behavior, 11*, 106408. https://doi.org/10.1016/j.chb.2020.106408

Kapoor, K. K., Tamilmani, K., Rana, N. P., Patil, P., Dwivedi, Y. K., & Nerur, S. (2018). Advances in social media research: Past, present and future. *Information Systems Frontiers, 20*(3), 531–558. https://doi.org/10.1007/s10796-017-9810-y

Kim, J., & Lee, J.-E. R. (2011). The Facebook paths to happiness: Effects of the number of Facebook friends and self-presentation on subjective wellbeing. *Cyberpsychology, Behavior, and Social Networking, 14*(6), 359–364. https://doi.org/10.1089/cyber.2010.0374

Lee, C., & Coughlin, J. F. (2015). Older adults' adults' adoption of technology: An integrated approach to identifying determinants and barriers. *Journal of Product Innovation Management, 32*(5), 747–759. https://doi.org/10.1111/jpim.12176

Lingard, L. (2019). Beyond the default colon: Effective use of quotes in qualitative research. *Perspectives on Medical Education, 8*(6), 360–364. https://doi.org/10.1007/s40037-019-00550-7

Matassi, M., Boczkowski, P. J., & Mitchelstein, E. (2019). Domesticating WhatsApp: Family, friends, work, and study in everyday communication. *New Media and Society.* https://doi.org/10.1177/1461444819841890

Mead, G., & Neves, B. (2018). Recursive approaches to technology adoption, families, and the life course: Actor network theory and strong structuration theory. In B. Neves, and C. Casimiro (Eds.), *Connecting Families? Information & Communication Technololgies, Generations and the Life Course* (pp. 41–57). Bristol University Press, Policy Press.

Miller, S. M. (2008). The effect of frequency and type of internet use on perceived social support and sense of wellbeing in individuals with spinal cord injury. *Rehabilitation Counseling Bulletin, 51*(3), 148–158. https://doi.org/10.1177/0034355207311315

Mubarak, F., & Nycyk, M. (2017). Teaching older people internet skills to mini-mize minimise grey digital divides: Developed and developing countries in focus. *Journal of Information, Communication and Ethics in Society, 15*(2), 165–178. https://doi.org/10.1108/JICES-06-2016-0022

Nabi, R. L., Prestin, A., & So, J. (2013). Facebook friends with (health) benefits? Exploring social network site use and perceptions of social support, stress, and wellbeing. *Cyberpsychology, Behavior, and Social Networking, 16*(10), 721–727. https://doi.org/10.1089/cyber.2012.0521

Nedelcu, M. (2017). Transnational grandparenting in the digital age: Mediated co-presence and childcare in the case of Romanian migrants in Switzerland and Canada. *European Journal of Ageing, 14*(4), 375–383. https://doi.org/10.1007/s10433-017-0436-1

Quan-Haase, A., Williams, C., Kicevski, M., Elueze, I., & Wellman, B. (2018). Dividing the grey divide: Deconstructing myths about older adults' adults' online activities, skills, and attitudes. *American Behavioral Scientist 62*(9) 1207–1228. https://doi.org/10.1177/0002764218777572

Reer, F., Tang, W. Y., & Quandt, T. (2019). Psychosocial wellbeing and social media engagement: The mediating roles of social comparison orientation and fear of missing out. *New Media & Society, 21*(7), 1486–1505. https://doi.org/10.1177/1461444818823719

Richards, D., Caldwell, P. H., & Go, H. (2015). Impact of social media on the health of children and young people. *Journal of Paediatrics and Child Health, 51*(12), 1152–1157. https://doi.org/10.1111/jpc.13023

Rosenthal, C. J. (1985). Kinkeeping in the familial division of labor. *Journal of Marriage and Family, 47*(4), 965–974. Retrieved January 24, 2020, from https://www.jstor.org.stable/352340

Schrock, A. R. (2015). Communicative affordances of mobile media: Portability, availability, locatability, and multimediality. *International Journal of Communication, 9*(1), 1229–1246. Retrieved April 21, 2021, from https://ijoc.org/index.php/ijoc/article/view/3288

Segrin, C., & Flora, J. (2018). *Family communication.* Routledge.

Shaker, S. F. (2018). A study of transnational communication among Iranian migrant women in Australia. *Journal of Immigrant and Refugee Studies, 16*(3), 293–312. https://doi.org/10.1080/15562948.2017.1283078

Share, M., Williams, C., & Kerrins, K. (2017). Displaying and performing: Polish transnational families in Ireland Skyping grandparents in Poland. *New Media & Society, 20*(8), 3011–3028. https://doi.org/10.1177/1461444817739272

Swist, T., Collin, P., McCormack, J., & Third, A. (2015). Social media and the wellbeing of children and young people: A literature review. Retrieved April 21, 2021, from https://researchdirect.westernsydney.edu.au/islandora/object/uws:36407/

Taipale, S. (2019). Intergenerational connections in digital families. *Springer.* https://doi.org/10.1007/978-3-030-11947-8

Tartari, E. (2015). Benefits and risks of children and adolescents using social media. *European Scientific Journal, 11*(13). Retrieved January 24, 2021, from https://core.ac.uk/reader/236413180

Taylor, S. E. (2011). Social support: A review. *The Oxford Handbook of Health Psychology.* https://doi.org/10.1093/oxfordhb/9780195342819.013.0009

van Boekel, L. C., Peek, S. T. M., & Luijkx, K. G. (2017). Diversity in older adults' adults' use of the internet: Identifying subgroups through latent class analysis. *Journal of Medical Internet Research, 19*(5), 1–11. https://doi.org/10.2196/JMIR.6853

Wherton, J., Sugarhood, P., Procter, R., et al. (2015). Designing technologies for social connection with older people. *Aging and the Digital Life Course, 3,* 107–124. https://doi.org/10.2307/j.ctt9qdb6b.12

Wolin, S. J., & Bennett, L. A. (1984). Family rituals. *Family Process, 23*(3), 401–420. https://doi.org/10.1111/j.1545-5300.1984.00401.x

Wright, K. B., Rosenberg, J., Egbert, N., Ploeger, N. A., Bernard, D. R., & King, S. (2013). Communication competence, social support, and depression among college students: A model of Facebook and face-to-face support network influence. *Journal of Health Communication, 18*(1), 41–57. https://doi.org/10.1080/10810730.2012.688250

Wulff, M., Champion, A., & Lobo, M. (2010). Household diversity and migration in mid-life: Understanding residential mobility among 45–64 year olds in Melbourne, Australia. *Population, Space and Place, 16,* 307–321. https://doi.org/10.1002/psp.553

Yang, C.-C. (2018). Social media as more than a peer space: College freshmen encountering parents on Facebook. *Journal of Adolescent Research, 33*(4), 442–469. https://doi.org/10.1177/0743558416659750

Yu, R., McCammon, R., Ellison, N., et al. (2015). The relationships that matter: Social network site use and social wellbeing among older adults in the United States of America. *Ageing and Society, 36*, 1826–1852. https://doi.org/10.1017/S0144686X15000677

Zhang, R. (2017). The stress-buffering effect of self-disclosure on Facebook: An examination of stressful life events, social support, and mental health among college students. *Computers in Human Behavior, 75*, 527–537. https://doi.org/10.1016/j.chb.2017.05.043

Zickuhr, K. & Madden, M. (2012). Older adults and internet use. *Pew Internet & American Life Project*. Retrieved January 24, 2021, from https://www.sainetz.at/dokumente/studien/Older_adults_and_internet_use_2012.pdf

Links Between Telehealth, Work, and Caring Responsibilities

Fiona Russo and Shalene Werth

Abstract Recent events related to the Covid-19 pandemic have seen changes to many aspects of life related to caring for children with disability or chronic health issues. Telehealth has gained traction in some contexts over time, but since the initial lockdowns associated with the Covid-19 pandemic it has been taken up at far greater rates and its desirability has increased. This chapter explores the positive impact of access to telehealth appointments with medical and professional service providers on work outcomes for caregivers who undertake paid work. It further demonstrates what this has meant for the work-care balance for the caregiver.

Keywords Employment · Caregiving · Telehealth · Health · Covid-19 · Work

---

F. Russo (✉) · S. Werth
University of Southern Queensland, Toowoomba, QLD, Australia
e-mail: fiona.russo@usq.edu.au

© The Author(s), under exclusive license to Springer Nature Switzerland AG 2022
T. Machin et al. (eds.), *Social Media and Technology Across the Lifespan*, Palgrave Studies in Cyberpsychology,
https://doi.org/10.1007/978-3-030-99049-7_6

Background

The concept of telehealth—also referred to as telemedicine or telepractice—is not new. It describes the use of platforms such as phone, videoconferencing, email, and technology-enabled home health monitoring in the delivery of healthcare services that would otherwise have required face-to-face contact in a clinical setting. In Australia, the tyranny of distance alone has seen a gradual increase in the use of telehealth to improve reach in rural and remote healthcare settings. Australian citizens and permanent residents access public health services through a socialised healthcare program (funded via levies paid through the individual income tax system) known as "Medicare", which provides low- or no-cost health care to patients. In the 2.5 years following the addition of telehealth services via Medicare in 2011, 115,000 video consultations were undertaken by specialist healthcare providers in underserved areas (Wade et al., 2014). This preparation may have positioned Australia well in its coordinated response to the 2020–2021 Covid-19 pandemic, which included the announcement on March 11 2020 of an AUD $2.4 bn health package to combat Covid-19. The Australian government earmarked $100 m to fund a new Medicare service to cover telehealth conversations via phone or video by general practitioners, specialists, nurses, and mental allied health workers. This new service was initially available for Covid-19 related consultations and then more widely to general and specialist health services for Australians at risk of Covid-19 infection (Fisk et al., 2020).

If we take a more global view, Bhatia (2021) found that a combination of poverty and/or distance in India, which was particularly hard-hit by Covid-19, has been a significant barrier for people in managing their health. Telehealth availability throughout the pandemic period acted as an enabler for specialist healthcare to reach communities in need quickly and efficiently, although Bhatia also acknowledged the limitation of insufficient telecommunications infrastructure in some areas. Interestingly, telehealth demonstrated benefits beyond those of infection control. Health care closer to home (or from home) that was made available without significant burden to the family also improved the general willingness of Indian people to engage with it. This is a story being repeated across the world as we become more aware of the health delivery systems response to Covid-19. The CONV2X 2020 conference reported a global increase in telehealth "visits" that represents 5000–17,500% (50–175x) of pre-COVID telehealth activity (Cenaj, 2021).

The work environment in Australia is regulated by legislation that prohibits discrimination against employees on the basis of family or carer's responsibilities and yet carers still need additional support to manage time away from work for medical appointments for a family member with disability or chronic illness. Workplace experiences for carers, throughout Covid-19 lockdowns and due to the use of telehealth appointments, show anecdotally that time away from the work desk for medical appointments has been minimised. The need to disclose personal information within the workplace in order to request time off has decreased and when combined with working from home in order to facilitate a telehealth appointment, there is minimal disruption to work on that day.

The impact of telehealth availability for family caregivers is not limited to the immediate health-related outcomes of remote service delivery for their loved ones. Dependents such as children or ageing parents with disabilities or chronic health conditions require a considerable level of care, support coordination, and advocacy that depletes the emotional, social, financial, and physical resources of unpaid family caregivers (Mason, 2019; Russo et al., 2020). The provision of telehealth services presents a less resource-intensive mode of delivery by limiting the travel time and cost and reducing the number of missed education/working hours associated with the coordination of clinical reviews and other appointments that could be offered remotely. It also provides a critical opportunity to lower the barriers to addressing their own self-care needs, which caregivers rarely prioritise due to time and energy constraints (Acton, 2002).

So… what does all this mean as the proverbial dust settles? How can the world's healthcare providers and funders take the learnings from this time and continue to pursue the benefits of telehealth in a post-pandemic landscape, and why should they? There are many studies extolling the virtues of telehealth for patients and even for the health delivery systems themselves. However, we also know that telehealth benefits extend beyond the patients and clinicians, also demonstrating positive caregiver and family outcomes which in turn lead to increased community and workplace participation and an even broader reach.

Methodology

An insider perspective brings to light issues that might be overlooked by outsider researchers. The concept of insiderness is one that is important. Authors of this chapter each have personal experiences of institutional responses to disability. Insiderness in relation to understanding emerging concepts is crucial for creating understanding for the broader community (Werth, 2013). Merton described insiders as having the role of being able to understand others in the same or similar situations. He stated, "you have to be one in order to understand one" (1972, p. 15). Merton also reports that:

> The outsider has neither been socialized in the group nor has engaged in the run of experience that makes up its life, and therefore cannot have the direct, intuitive sensitivity that alone makes empathetic understanding possible. (Merton, 1972, p. 15)

In the process of examining the literature on telehealth and balancing work and care for a family member with a disability, we have applied the lens of an insider in order to bring to light issues and possibilities related to these topics.

This narrative literature is integrative in nature. We are, from an insider perspective, looking at two sides of an issue that has not been thoroughly examined. With the advent of the Covid-19 pandemic there has been a move towards using technology as a more flexible part of a healthcare routine. This was required as part of the infection control measures that were important for containing the epidemic. An integrative approach to examining literature presents an opportunity to "generate new knowledge about a topic by reviewing, critiquing and synthesizing representative literature on a topic in such a way that new ... perspectives on the topic are generated" (Torraco, 2016, p. 62). Approaching this by developing a narrative literature review allows us to explore the topic using an insider lens that provides a way to search far more broadly and examine research questions that may not have been explored previously. Noble and Smith point out that narrative overviews are very useful for providing a "comprehensive synthesis of evidence" (2018, p. 39). They also state that a narrative overview can be "used to synthesize information into a user-friendly format and present a broad perspective on a subject, its development and management" (Noble & Snith, 2018, p. 39).

The two areas of research that we will examine include workplace flexibility for working caregivers of people with disability, and telehealth and related technologies for the healthcare setting. Unique circumstances have brought this topic to the fore because lockdown or social distancing measures undertaken by most countries at some point during 2020 and 2021 have provided a catalyst for change. Telehealth has previously only been undertaken in rural and isolated settings where access to healthcare professionals is difficult due to distance.

The Scale and Impact of Caring in Australia

There are 2.65 million informal caregivers in Australia (Australian Government, 2018), representing 10.8% of the total population. Seven in ten of these family caregivers are women caring for children, spouses, or ageing parents with chronic health issues and/or disabilities. Over a third of primary caregivers are also living with their own disabilities, twice the rate of non-carers. Perhaps most alarmingly, more than half of the caregiver households appear among the lowest two quintiles of household income, a rate double that of the non-carer population. These statistics illustrate the scale and impact of informal (non-professional) caregiving in Australia. They paint a picture of family caregiving responsibilities falling largely to women who are more likely to experience poverty and disability themselves. This clearly identifies a population of caregivers who are within the age range for active workforce participation—parents caring for children with complex health needs/disability and adult children caring for ageing parents—and these populations are the primary focus of this writing.

There is little data available that classifies the disabilities prevalent among family caregivers. However, there is a variety of contemporary literature that describes negative mental health experiences in caregivers, especially when caring for children with disabilities or poor medical prognoses (Barros et al., 2019; Cetinbakis et al., 2020; Javalkar et al., 2017; Juntunen et al., 2018; Marquis et al., 2019; Masefield et al., 2020). Many of these studies are focussed on mothers as primary caregivers, but one recent study of fatherhood in the context of childhood disability presented similar findings (Steinour & Green, 2019). Many informal caregivers are experiencing anxiety, stress, and depression stemming from their role and further compounded by feelings of isolation within their local communities (Cetinbakis et al., 2020; Marquis et al., 2019; Toledano-Toledano & de la Rubia, 2018). Lower rates of community engagement and workplace participation are common among parent caregivers (Brannan et al., 2018; Brown & Clark, 2017; Ejiri & Matsuzawa, 2019; Sellmaier et al., 2020) and are likely and logical contributors to these negative psychosocial experiences. Even in cases where caregivers are able to be active in the workforce, a lack of organisational support for the caregiving role presents significant barriers to career progression and overall work satisfaction (Stefanidis & Strogilos, 2021).

Juggling the dual roles of work and care has been a task that (generally) women have undertaken. These responsibilities have become complicated by various factors including caring for a family member with a disability or chronic illness (Barusch & Spaid, 1989; Case, 2000; Folbre, 2006; Hervey & Shaw, 1998), access to appropriate medical care and what accommodations their workplace is prepared to provide for them to facilitate medical and professional appointments.

Work and Care

Disadvantage felt by individuals with caring responsibilities may be caused by an inability to access the working hours they desire. In Australia, a parent or other person who has primary responsibility for the care of a child who is school age or younger has a legal entitlement to request flexible working arrangements under the *Fair Work Act 2009 (Cwlth)*. However, this request may be denied on the basis of reasonable business grounds. Caring responsibilities where flexibility is not available may result in caregivers working more hours than they would prefer. This has the potential to disadvantage workers in the workplace as, generally, "part-time workers (relative to full-time workers) have low expectations regarding the quality of their job" (Jocoy, 2003, p. 37), hence their ability to access satisfying work may be impaired.

Vickers, Parris, and Bailey (2004) noted that women tended to shoulder a greater responsibility for caring for children with health issues than partners, even where they were also undertaking paid work. They also observed that the women responsible for caring for children with disability were usually the "first point of call for their child's needs, whether at home, at school or with medical requirements such as doctors' visits…" (Vickers et al., 2004, p. 43). Parents in Green's (2007) study entitled "We're Tired, Not Sad" reported that their emotional resources were less impacted than their socio-cultural ones. They spoke about the burden of paperwork and the intensity of negotiations with medical and education professionals associated with having a child with complex needs (Green, 2007).

Anecdotal evidence (corroborated by the lived experience of the authors) clearly identifies the impact of a single specialist review appointment on day-to-day family life. These appointments often necessitate a day off school and work, long travel times and significant cost for parking and transport and result in frustration when the appointment itself might easily have been replaced by a phone call or video consultation. "The mother, even if she works outside the home, is usually the one to take the child to the required medical and professional appointments" (Vickers & Parris, 2005, p. 100), further compounding the perception of mothers in the workplace as being less available for or less committed to their careers.

In a discussion regarding work–family balance, Brown and Clark (2017) note that flexible work hours are important for families of children with a disability. They go on to say that flexible working hours are also critical to enable working mothers attend medical appointments that can only be scheduled during business hours (Brown & Clark, 2017). The complex interplay of medical requirements and workplace expectations is difficult to negotiate unless there are additional workplace accommodations available for parents in this position. Mothers in one Australian study of parental caregiving cited this issue often, one stating:

> I was working part-time after having children and full-time before that, in management consulting" ... "then, due to [child] having her diagnosis and flexibility needed in the workplace for me having to drop the ball at the last minute because she's been sick or the childcare centre has called me... or because of appointments. I ended up getting discriminated against at work and lost my job when they restructured. (Russo, 2019, p. 72)

In another study, Brown and Clark (2017) note that parents who felt that they had good workplace support had lower levels of strain and higher levels of professional efficacy. The advantages for workplaces, who provide additional levels of understanding and flexibility for individuals who require help with the circumstances of disability and chronic illness, are valuable for the workplace environment (Werth, 2015).

Informal Caregiving and the Role of Telehealth

As highlighted above, one of the most common factors relating to limited workforce and community participation rates among parent caregivers is a perception of reduced availability due to the demands of the caring role (Cetinbakis et al., 2020; Ejiri & Matsuzawa, 2019; Martel et al., 2021; Toledano-Toledano & de la Rubia, 2018). One such factor is the time and effort expended in the management and coordination of appointments relating to their family member/'s needs. Brown and Clark (2017)'s review of literature cited a number of studies in which caregivers spoke about doctors, schools, and other service providers scheduling appointments inflexibly during regular business hours, and this coupled with a lack of flexible workplace practices presents a significant barrier to caregiver employment. Telehealth is well placed to offer some mitigation of this barrier by enabling families to attend virtual appointments where it is clinically appropriate. This approach has the potential to increase workforce participation among caregivers, resulting in greater earning capacity and improved standards of living among households in this sector.

The benefits of telehealth for family caregivers are not only related to workforce participation. A pre-pandemic review of literature pertaining to telehealth in the context of people with complex social care needs (Davies et al., 2013) demonstrated positive outcomes for informal (family) caregivers such as an increase in the reach of community supports and education for caregivers that resulted in reduced isolation, depressions, stress and anxiety, and an overall reduction in reported caregiver strain. An earlier study by Mahoney et al. (2008) explored the role of workplace-based telehealth in improving outcomes for patients, caregivers, and employers alike. Their intervention was aimed at adult caregivers of elderly parents and demonstrated significant positive outcomes relating to the caregivers' energy available for work, attention to detail in work projects, higher workplace output in terms of both quality and quantity, and overall reductions in caring-related stress and anxiety (p. 231). They also demonstrated that the telehealth intervention did not replace or reduce the quality of direct care and communication between caregivers and their elderly parents throughout the study period.

The Disabling Effects of Society

Disability research, as it relates to workforce participation, draws on theory from various traditions, including disability, sociology, psychology, industrial relations, and management. In the disability literature, the medical model and social model of disability have been widely researched (Barnes, 2000; Donoghue, 2003; Oliver & Barnes, 2010). The medical model focuses on "individual medical conditions as the causes of disability" (Smith, 2008, p. 15). This perspective was a dominant feature in disability research in the 1950s. In the 1960s and 1970s, the Disability Rights Movement in Britain was instrumental in the development of a new model, known as the social model of disability (Oliver & Barnes, 2010). This model was endorsed as part of the "resistance to social oppression and the medical model of disability" (Peters et al., 2009, p. 543) and was described by Oliver and Barnes thus, "while impairment may impose personal restrictions, disability is created by hostile cultural, social and environmental barriers" (2010, p. 552).

Other models have been advanced at different times, the World Health Organisation (WHO) has used the biopsychosocial model for its Second International Classification of Functioning Disability and Health (ICF) since 2001. WHO noted that:

> On their own neither model [social model or medical model] is adequate, although both are partially valid. Disability is a complex phenomena that is both a problem at the level of a person's body, and a complex and primarily social phenomena. Disability is always an interaction between features of the person and features of the overall context in which the person lives, but some aspects of disability are almost entirely internal to the person, while another aspect is almost entirely external… [A] more useful model of disability might be called the biopsychosocial model. (World Health Organisation, 2002, p. 9)

WHO stated, in relation to the biopsychosocial model, that "a better model of disability, is one that synthesizes what is true in the medical and social models, without making the mistakes each makes in reducing the whole, complex notion of disability to one of its aspects" (World Health Organisation, 2002, p. 9). In Australia, the organisation People with Disability (PWD) is an advocacy group, broadly termed a cross-disability disabled people's organisation. They assess that the social model of disability is important in developing an understanding of impairment and socially constructed disability.

The social model seeks to change society in order to accommodate people living with impairment; it does not seek to change persons with impairment to accommodate society. It supports the view that people with disability have a right to be fully participating citizens on an equal basis with other. (ADCET, 2021)

Disability activism in Australia employs the social model as the basis of its advocacy. Meekosha and Dowse (1997) state that: "there is an implicit assumption that disability is an individual attribute, adhering to the strictly medical model of disability, rather than seeing disability as socially constructed – a form of oppression" (p. 64). The history of the treatment of people with disability centred around deficit social attitudes and the medical model. In Australia, the focus for achieving improved outcomes for individuals with disability relies on the use of the social model. This individualistic [medical] model of disability focuses on curing disability in individuals, while a sociology of disability allows for an understanding of how disability arises from structural barriers" (Sang et al., 2021, p. 3). Removing structural impediments to success for children with disability as they grow up and providing meaningful work opportunities for their caregivers contribute directly to this.

Discussion and Conclusions

The intersections between work, care, disability or chronic illness, and telehealth are important to consider. Advocates in this space tend to be experts in individual fields and might miss the significance of looking at all of these. Experts arrive at the issues with their own perspectives about "how things should turn out". Managers in workplaces tend to have preconceived ideas of what an ideal worker looks like for their workplace, they might be reluctant to provide accommodations for employees who have caring responsibilities. Managers also buy into the "medical model" by exhibiting attitudes that expect that there should be an end-point to any disability or illness that means that an employee needs accommodations from their workplace. In this kind of work environment, the use of telehealth can assist employees by minimising the time that they need to take away from the work for medical appointments. Alternately, workers who work for supportive employers can also benefit from the accessibility to health care that telehealth readily provides.

Medical professionals approach the interactions between work, care, disability, and telehealth, with the expectation that quality health care takes precedence over everything else. For some medical professionals that means that telehealth is a less desirable option for the provision of health care (see Jansen et al., 2020; Lipman, 2011 and others). There is also an expectation that others such as employers will provide flexibility for employees who are caring for a child with disability, because of the perceived precedence that the medical model takes over all other expectations of work and life. However, this may not actually be the case in practice. The variable expectations of what a caregiver will do and what their priorities will be places them in the unenviable position of having to choose between work, care, and medical expectations. This creates what Barbara Pocock (2003) refers to as a "work-life collision". She states that this "is about the interactions between spheres of work, gender relations, consumption, community, and family" (Pocock, 2003, p. 3). Within this model, we see issues such as the increasing number of women who are undertaking paid work and who are seeking a career and a higher level of wages, the increasing number of dual-income households with dependents, and lesser participation in the community (Pocock, 2003). At the same, women are experiencing a gendered distribution of domestic work and care and pressure to undertake most of this, the precarious nature of part-time and casual work, and fewer protections in the legal framework of employment (Pocock, 2003).

What this means is that caregivers, who are mostly women, face a variety of pressures and difficulties in their home and work lives. Currently, it appears from the literature and from anecdotal evidence that women are navigating helpful/less helpful workplaces; medical professionals who may or may not be willing to be a part of a disability community which is essential; household and disability/health-related administration; travel, where there is no option for a telehealth consultation; and jobs where carers' leave may not available. Telehealth is not the entire answer to these issues, but it should be considered as an option that prevents the caregiver from taking extensive time away from work. Mahoney et al.'s (2008) research on? workplace-based telehealth found that benefits of the program included increased carer's energy available for work, improved attention to detail, increased productivity, and reductions in stress and anxiety.

It is worth noting that people with disability are themselves underemployed in the Australian context, with less than half being active in the workforce vs more than 80% of those without disability (Australian Government, 2018). Although there are other impairment-related factors at play here, flexible workplace practices and telehealth offerings may also assist to reduce this disparity and improve employment outcomes in people with disabilities and chronic health conditions. Jeste et al. (2020, p. 825) state that "telehealth may provide opportunities for delivery of care and education in a sustainable way, not only as [COVID-19] restrictions endure but after they have been lifted". Improved creativity is touted as another benefit of telehealth as it has the potential to change the way work takes place (Schur et al., 2020).

Our own reflections are therefore that telehealth should not be returned to the fringes of health service delivery at the end of the pandemic. We must acknowledge the considerable value that exists beyond simple infection control and promote and pursue these far-reaching benefits by furthering support for telehealth delivery beyond the Covid-19 response frameworks.

References

Acton, G. J. (2002). Health-promoting self-care in family caregivers. *Western Journal of Nursing Research, 24*(1), 73–86.

Australian Disability Clearinghouse in Education and Training (ADCET). (2021). Disability in the Social and Political Context. Retrieved from October 11, 2021. https://www.adcet.edu.au/inclusive-teaching/understanding-disability/social-political-context#Ref

Australian Government. (2018). *Disability, Ageing and Carers Australia: Summary of Findings*. ABS Retrieved from October 11, 2021. https://www.abs.gov.au/statistics/health/disability/disability-ageing-and-carers-australia-summary-findings/latest-release#key-statistics

Barnes, C. (2000). A working social model? Disabiliity, work and disability politics in the 21st century. *Critical Social Policy, 20*(4), 441–457.

Barros, A. L. O., de Gutierrez, G. M., Barros, A. O., & Santos, M. T. B. R. (2019). Quality of life and burden of caregivers of children and adolescents with disabilities. *Special Care in Dentistry, 39*(4), 380–388.

Barusch, A. S., & Spaid, W. M. (1989). Gender differences in caregiving: Why do wives report greater burden? *The Gerontologist, 29*(5), 667–676.

Bhatia, R. (2021). Telehealth and COVID-19: Using technology to accelerate the curve on access and quality healthcare for citizens in India. *Technology in Society, 64*, 101465.

Brannan, A. M., Brennan, E. M., Sellmaier, C., & Rosenzweig, J. M. (2018). Employed parents of children receiving mental health services: Caregiver strain and work–life integration. *Families in Society, 99*(1), 29–44.

Brown, T. J., & Clark, C. (2017). *Employed parents of children with disabilities and work family life balance: A literature review.* Paper presented at the Child & Youth Care Forum.

Case, M. A. (2000). How high the Apple Pie-A few troubling questions about where, why, and how the burden of care for children should be shifted. *Chicago-Kent Law Review, 76,* 1753.

Cenaj, T. (2021). COVID-19 and the Digital Transformation of Health Care. *Telehealth and Medicine Today.*

Cetinbakis, G., Bastug, G., & Ozel-Kizil, E. (2020). Factors contributing to higher caregiving burden in Turkish mothers of children with autism spectrum disorders. *International Journal of Developmental Disabilities, 66*(1), 46–53.

Davies, A., Rixon, L., & Newman, S. (2013). Systematic review of the effects of telecare provided for a person with social care needs on outcomes for their informal carers. *Health & Social Care in the Community, 21*(6), 582–597.

Donoghue, C. (2003). Challenging the authority of the medical definition of disability: An analysis of the resistance to the social constructionist paradigm. *Disability & Society, 18*(2), 199–208.

Ejiri, K., & Matsuzawa, A. (2019). Factors associated with employment of mothers caring for children with intellectual disabilities. *International Journal of Developmental Disabilities, 65*(4), 239–247.

Fisk, M., Livingstone, A., & Pit, S. W. (2020). Telehealth in the context of COVID-19: changing perspectives in Australia, the United Kingdom, and the United States. *Journal of Medical Internet Research, 22*(6), e19264.

Folbre, N. (2006). Measuring care: Gender, empowerment, and the care economy. *Journal of Human Development, 7*(2), 183–199.

Green, S. E. (2007). "We're tired, not sad": Benefits and burdens of mothering a child with a disability. *Social Science & Medicine, 64*(1), 150–163.

Hervey, T., & Shaw, J. (1998). Women, work and care: Women's dual role and double burden in EC sex equality law. *Journal of European Social Policy, 8*(1), 43–63.

Jansen, M., Helen, I., Gillam, L., Sharwood, E., Preisz, A., Basu, S., Delaney, C., McDougall, R., Johnston, C., Isaacs, D., & Lister, P. (2020). Ethical considerations for paediatrics during the Covid-19 pandemic: A discussion paper from the Australian Paediatric Clinical Ethics Collaboration. *Journal of Paediatrics and Child Health, 56,* 847–851.

Javalkar, K., Rak, E., Phillips, A., Haberman, C., Ferris, M., & Van Tilburg, M. (2017). Predictors of caregiver burden among mothers of children with chronic conditions. *Children, 4*(5), 39.

Jeste, S., Hyde, C., Distefano, C., Halladay, A., Ray, S., Porath, M., & Thurm, A. (2020). Changes in access to educational and healthcare services for individuals with intellectual and developmental disabilities during Covid-19 restrictions. *Journal of Intellectual Disability Research, 64* (Part II), 825–833.

Jocoy, C. L. (2003). Vying for hearts and minds: Emotional labour as management control. *Labour & Industry, 13*(3), 72–52.

Juntunen, K., Salminen, A. L., Törmäkangas, T., Tillman, P., Leinonen, K., & Nikander, R. (2018). Perceived burden among spouse, adult child, and parent caregivers. *Journal of Advanced Nursing, 74*(10), 2340–2350.

Lipman, M. (2011). The doctor will Skype you now. *Consumer Reports, 76*(8), 12.

Mahoney, D. M., Mutschler, P. H., Tarlow, B., & Liss, E. (2008). Real world implementation lessons and outcomes from the Worker Interactive Networking (WIN) project: Workplace-based online caregiver support and remote monitoring of elders at home. *Telemedicine and e-Health, 14*(3), 224–234.

Marquis, S., Hayes, M. V., & McGrail, K. (2019). Factors affecting the health of caregivers of children who have an intellectual/developmental disability. *Journal of Policy and Practice in Intellectual Disabilities, 16*(3), 201–216.

Martel, A., Day, K., Jackson, M. A., & Kaushik, S. (2021). Beyond the pandemic: The role of the built environment in supporting people with disabilities work life. *Archnet-IJAR: International Journal of Architectural Research.*

Masefield, S. C., Prady, S. L., Sheldon, T. A., Small, N., Jarvis, S., & Pickett, K. E. (2020). The caregiver health effects of caring for young children with developmental disabilities: a meta-analysis. *Maternal and Child Health Journal*, 1–14.

Mason, N. F. (2019). Health Information Seeking as a Coping Strategy to Reduce the Stress of Informal Caregivers of Individuals with Alzheimer's Disease and Other Forms of Dementia.

Merton, R. K. (1972). Insiders and outsiders: A chapter in the sociology of knowledge. *The American Journal of Sociology, 78*(1), 9–47.

Meekosha, H., & Dowse, L. (1997). Enabling citizenship: Gender, disability and citizenship in Australia. *Feminist Review, 57*, 49–72.

Noble, H., & Smith, J. (2018). Reviewing the literature: choosing a review design. *Evidence Based Nursing, 21*(2).

Oliver, M., & Barnes, C. (2010). Disability studies, disabled people and the struggle for inclusion. *British Journal of Sociology and Education, 31*(5), 547–560.

Peters, S., Gabel, S., & Symeonidou, S. (2009). Resistance, transformation and the politics of hope: Imagining a way forward for the disabled people's movement. *Disability & Society, 24*(5), 543–556.

Pocock, B. (2003). *The Work/Life Collision.* The Federation Press.

Russo, F. F. (2019). *Supporting the development of advocacy in the parent/carers of Queensland children with disability* (Doctoral dissertation, University of Southern Queensland).

Russo, F., Brownlow, C., & Machin, T. (2020). Parental experiences of engaging with the National Disability Insurance Scheme for their children: A systematic literature review. *Journal of Disability Policy Studies, 32*, 1044207320943607.

Sang, K., Calvard, T., & Remnant, J. (2021). *Disability and academic careers: Using the social relational model to reveal the role of human resource management practices in creating disability* (pp. 1–19). Employment and Society, Online first.

Schur, L. A., Ameri, M., & Kruse, D. (2020). Telework after COVID: a 'silver lining' for workers with disabilities? *Journal of Occupational Rehabilitation*, Online 6 November 2020.

Sellmaier, C., Stewart, L. M., & Brennan, E. M. (2020). Workforce participation of parents of children and youth with mental health difficulties: The impact of community services and supports. *Community, Work & Family, 23*(5), 534–555.

Smith, S. R. (2008). Competing interpretations of the medical and social models. In K. Kristiansen, T. Shakespeare, and S. Vehmas (Eds.), *Arguing about disability: philosophical perspectives*. Routledge.

Stefanidis, A., & Strogilos, V. (2021). Perceived organizational support and work engagement of employees with children with disabilities. *Personnel Review, 50*(1), 186–206.

Steinour, H., & Green, S. E. (2019). *"More than a Parent, You're a Caregiver": Narratives of fatherhood in families of adult sons and daughters with life-long disabilities*. Emerald Publishing Limited.

Toledano-Toledano, F., & de la Rubia, J. M. (2018). Factors associated with anxiety in family caregivers of children with chronic diseases. *BioPsychoSocial Medicine, 12*(1), 1–10.

Torraco, R. (2016). Writing integrative reviews of the literature: Methods and purposes. *International Journal of Adult Vocational Education and Technology, 7*(3), 62–70.

Vickers, M., & Parris, M. A. (2005). Towards ending the silence: Working women caring for children with chronic illness. *Employee Responsibilities and Rights Journal, 17*(2), 91–108.

Vickers, M., Parris, M., & Bailey, J. (2004). Working mothers of children with chronic illness. *Early Childhood Australia, 29*(1).

Wade, V., Soar, J., & Gray, L. (2014). Uptake of telehealth services funded by Medicare in Australia. *Australian Health Review, 38*(5), 528–532.

Werth, S. (2013). *An investigation of the interaction of chronically ill women and their working environments*. (PhD), Griffith University, Brisbane.

Werth, S. (2015). Managerial attitudes: Influences on workforce outcomes for working women with chronic illness. *Economic and Labour Relations Review, 26*(2), 296–313.

World Health Organisation. (2002). *Towards a Common Language for Functioning, Disability and Health: ICF.* (WHO/EIP/GPE/CAS/01.3). Geneva. Retrieved from October 11, 2021. http://www.who.int/classifications/icf/training/icfbeginnersguide.pdf

The Effects of Facebook-Based Social Support on Health Across Metropolitan and Regional Australians

John Gilmour, Carla Jeffries, Tanya Machin, and Charlotte Brownlow

Abstract Facebook has become an important part of building and maintaining relationships and an increasingly integral part of our lives at all developmental stages. Using Facebook to connect with friends and family can provide greater perceptions of social support, providing a buffer between life stress and physical and mental health outcomes. It has been hypothesised that geographically diverse communities may use Facebook to compensate for limited opportunities to access face-to-face social support. This study examines the role of Facebook-based social support on physical and mental health concerns (mental distress, dissatisfaction with life, and physical illness) across two samples of Australian adult Facebook users (209 living in metropolitan areas, 158 living regionally). Greater levels of Facebook-based social support predicted lower levels of health concerns in a metropolitan-based sample. No association between Facebook-based social support and health concerns was found in

---

J. Gilmour (✉) · C. Jeffries · T. Machin · C. Brownlow
University of Southern Queensland, Toowoomba, QLD, Australia
e-mail: john.stephen.gilmour@gmail.com

the regional sample. This result shows that the use of Facebook as a mechanism for social support, and its effects on health, vary across geographical locations, and appears to be mainly found in a metropolitan population.

Keywords Facebook · Social support · Mental health · Regional health · Social media

Introduction

Facebook, as a social networking site, is immensely popular, with approximately 65% of Australians having a Facebook account (Crowling, 2016; Sensis, 2017; Statistica, 2020). Research has already shown that perceptions of social support from interactions on Facebook can be beneficial to health (Gilmour et al., 2019; Kim & Lee, 2011; Nabi et al., 2013). Recent work examining the use of social media as a mechanism for social supporthas found that Facebook can improve perceptions of social support, which can then reduce mental distress and physical illness (Gilmour et al., 2019). However, the location of the user (i.e., living in a major city vs. living in a regional area), and the effect this can have on Facebook as a mechanism for social support have yet to be examined. Thus, this research investigates the use of Facebook to enhance perceived social support across metropolitan and regional communities, and the potential positive effects on physical and mental health that this type of support may provide. While the differential uses across geographical locations may be seen across the lifespan, this chapter will focus on adults.

According to the Australian Institute of Health and Welfare, the physical and mental health outcomes for Australians living in regional areas (i.e. located away from major cities and close to moderate population centres) has been shown to be significantly worse than persons who live in a metropolitan area (AIHW, 2016, 2019; Bourke et al., 2012; Kelly et al., 2010). Mental health issues such as anxiety and depression for those who live in regional areas occur at much higher rates than those in major Australian cities (AIHW, 2016, 2019). Additionally, physical health outcomes are similarly worse for Australians living regionally, including increased risks for alcohol and drug abuse, and decreased positive health activities (AIHW, 2016, 2019). The lack of access to facilities, the increased stress of poor economic opportunities, the stigma around mental health, and social isolation are all major factors in poorer health outcomes for regional Australians (Alston, 2012; Fraser et al., 2002; Wrigley et al., 2005).

A predictor in better physical and mental health outcomes has consistently been shown to be social support (Campbell et al., 2011; Cohen & Wills, 1985; Luszczynska et al., 2013). Social support is the extent to which a person feels there is a social network available for them to draw on for emotional and practical support (Campbell et al., 2011; Cohen & Wills, 1985; Luszczynska et al., 2013). Research has demonstrated people with greater perceived social support will experience fewer mental health issues and better physical health than those with less perceived social support (Campbell et al., 2011; Cohen & Wills, 1985; Luszczynska et al., 2013). Increased social support has been found to predict lower levels of physical illness and mental distress, as well as higher levels of life satisfaction (Campbell et al., 2011; Cohen & Wills, 1985; Luszczynska et al., 2013; Nabi et al., 2013).

Social support also moderates the negative effect that stress has on physical and mental health (Cohen & Wills, 1985; Li et al., 2015). Stress (i.e. the feeling of mental strain or pressure) can be caused by both internal and external factors, such as negative self-perception, or job loss (Sapolsky, 1994; Zhang, 2017). The level of social support an individual perceives they can draw on, rather than the actual social support they receive, often buffers the individual from the negative effects of stress with this effect known as the buffering hypothesis (Cohen & Wills, 1985; Zhang, 2017). The mechanism behind this buffering effect is known as stress and coping theory, which posits life events are stressful only to the extent that an individual appraises the severity of, and their inability to cope with, the event (Cohen & Wills, 1985; Thoits, 1986; Zhang, 2017). Specifically, an individual with greater perceived social support feels they have greater practical and emotional interpersonal resources to draw on to both resolve the source of the stress, and to gain emotional support while under that source of stress (Wallston et al., 1983; Zhang, 2017).

One of the potential barriers to accessing face-to-face social support from relevant or like-minded groups and individuals in regional communities is the relative distance between individuals and population centres (Koopman et al., 2001; Lauckner & Hutchinson, 2016; Vyavaharkar et al., 2010). This distance can lead to social isolation and loneliness, which, in turn, can affect mental health (Alston, 2012; Kawachi & Berkman, 2001). However, with the introduction of contemporary, internet-based communications, such as social media, it is likely that new methods of drawing on social support have been incorporated into many regional communities, potentially mitigating the effects of life challenges.

Social support drawn from Facebook has been associated with improved physical and mental health, and greater life satisfaction and well-being (Gilmour et al., 2019; Kim & Lee, 2011; Nabi et al., 2013). Facebook use, including time spent on Facebook and number of Facebook Friends are associated with greater perceptions of Facebook-based social support (Gilmour et al., 2019; Kim & Lee, 2011; Nabi et al., 2013), although overuse of Facebook can have negative health outcomes (Frost & Rickwood, 2017). Studies have found that Facebook-based social support can predict lower levels of perceived stress, physical illness, and mental health (Kim & Lee, 2011; Nabi et al., 2013), with evidence suggesting social support drawn from Facebook can be used to supplement reduced social inclinations or opportunities to access face-to-face social support (Indian & Grieve, 2014). Thus researchers have suggested that persons living in more geographically-isolated areas could potentially utilise Facebook to access online social support, and thus improve mental health (Indian & Grieve, 2014). However, most of the studies examining Facebook-based social support only draw from metropolitan or student samples (Gilmour et al., 2019).

This chapter explores the research question "is there a difference in the effects of social support drawn from Facebook on physical and mental health outcomes for metropolitan and regional Australians?" Therefore, overall, this chapter aims to evaluate the effects of Facebook-based social support on health outcomes, such as mental distress, dissatisfaction with life, and physical illness, for persons living in metropolitan and regional areas of Australia.

Drawing from the reviewed literature several hypotheses were developed. Firstly, it is hypothesised that time spent on Facebook and number of Facebook Friends will be positively related to Facebook-based social support (H1). Additionally, it is hypothesised that perceived life stress, and time spent on Facebook will have a positive relationship with physical and mental health concerns (H2a and H2b, respectively). To incorporate the buffering hypothesis, it is hypothesised that Facebook-based social support will mediate the relationship between perceived life stress, and physical and mental health concerns (H3). Finally, it has been suggested in previous research that persons living in geographically isolated areas may use Facebook to supplement for reduced opportunities to access face-to-face social support (Indian & Grieve, 2014). As such, it is also hypothesised that the effect of Facebook-based social support on physical and mental health concerns will be strongest in the regional sample when compared to the metropolitan sample (H4).

Methods
Participants and Procedure

Participants were recruited via an online survey, between August 2018 and March 2019. Recruitment methods of members of the general public were performed via acquaintance networks, social media advertising (i.e. Facebook, LinkedIn, and Twitter), and in-person at public events in regional communities. In addition, an undergraduate Psychology student pool at a regional Australian university was utilised. Participants were offered either entry in a cash prize draw (i.e. $50 gift voucher) or course credit following the completion of the survey. Participants had to be current Facebook users, reside in Australia, and be over 18 years of age. Three hundred and seventy-four participants were initially recruited; however, seven participants were removed for incomplete or implausible responses, leaving a total sample of 367 participants.

Measures

Demographics
To categorise location (i.e. metropolitan or regional community), participants provided their postcode as well as distance from their residence to the nearest population centre. This enabled categorisation as either a metropolitan or regional residence based on the Australian Statistical Geography Standard (ASGS) Remoteness Areas criteria (ABS, 2016; AIHW, 2004). Demographic information, including age and gender were also collected (see Table 1 for sample descriptive statistics).

Facebook Use
Facebook use was measured as self-reported time spent on Facebook per day (recorded as minutes and hours) and number of Facebook Friends on the participants' account. Due to extreme non-normality, number of Facebook Friends was transformed logarithmically.

Table 1 Demographic information of both the regional and metropolitan samples

	Metropolitan (n = 209)	Regional (n = 158)
Age	36.28 (SD = 12.62)	36.32 (SD = 13.40)
Gender		
Male	52 (24.9%)	30 (19.0%)
Female	157 (75.1%)	128 (81.0%)
Hours spent on Facebook (per day)	1.50 (SD = 1.57)	1.65 (SD = 163)
No. of Facebook friends	310.00 (SD = 293.02)	384.14 (SD = 464.95)
Device most used to engage Facebook		
Mobile device	174 (83.3%)	125 (79.1%)
Personal computer	18 (8.6%)	20 (12.7%)
Tablet	16 (7.7%)	12 (7.6%)
Computer at school/work	1 (0.4%)	1 (0.6%)
Level of employment		
Full-time	106 (50.7%)	55 (34.8%)
Part-time	27 (12.9%)	36 (22.8%)
Casual	23 (11.0%)	29 (18.4%)
Student	44 (21.1%)	27 (17.1%)
Not employed	9 (4.3%)	11 (7.0%)

Facebook-Based Social Support

A modified version of the Interpersonal Support Evaluation List–Short Form (ISEL-SF), informed by the design utilised in Indian and Grieve (2014), was used to measure Facebook-based social support. Participants responded to items using a 4-point Likert scale (0 = "*definitely false*" to 3 = "*definitely true*"). An example item was: "*When I need suggestions on how to deal with a personal problem, I know someone on Facebook I can turn to*". The modified ISEL-SF showed excellent internal consistency in this sample ($\alpha = 0.90$) and has been used in previous studies that examine Facebook-based social support (Indian & Grieve, 2014; Kim & Lee, 2011).

Perceived Life Stress

Perceived life stress was measured by the 10-item Perceived Stress Scale (PSS; Cohen et al., 1983) which assesses an individual's perception of the stability of their life, as well as their ability to deal with stressful situations (Cohen et al., 1983; Hewitt et al., 1992). Participants were asked to rate how often they have thought or felt a certain way, such as "*In the last* month, how often have you felt that you were unable to control the important things in your life?", on a 5-point Likert scale (0 = "never" to 4 = "very often"). The PSS showed good internal consistency ($\alpha = 0.89$), and has been used in previous studies exploring Facebook-based social support as a measure of global perceived stress (Wright, 2012; Wright et al., 2013).

Mental Distress
Mental distress was measured using the Depression Anxiety Stress Scale-21 (DASS-21). The DASS-21 is a 21-item self-report questionnaire used to measure an individual's levels of depression, anxiety, and stress (Osman et al., 2012). The DASS-21 requires participants to rate how much each item relates to them in the previous week (e.g., "*I felt down-hearted and blue*"), using a 4-point Likert scale, ranging from 0 ("*never*") to 3 ("*almost always*"). The DASS-21 showed excellent internal consistency in this sample ($\alpha = 0.95$). The DASS-21 has shown strong construct and discriminant validity in previous studies (Henry & Crawford, 2005; Osman et al., 2012).

Dissatisfaction with Life
Dissatisfaction with life was assessed by the Satisfaction with Life Scale (SWLS). The SWLS is a 5-item self-report questionnaire used to globally measure the extent to which a person experiences contentment with their current life circumstances (Diener et al., 1985). Individual rates the extent to which they agree with statements, such as "*In most ways, my life is close to my ideal*", on a 7-point Likert scale (1 = "*strongly disagree*" to 7 = "*strongly agree*"). The SWLS showed good-to-excellent internal consistency ($\alpha = 0.89$) in this sample and has shown strong convergent and divergent validity (Diener et al., 1985; Pavot & Diener, 1993, 2008).

Physical Illness
Physical illness was measured using the Physical Illness Measure (PIM). The PIM is a five-item scale that assesses how often an individual experiences physical illness sensations and symptoms (Jackson et al., 2002). Participants were asked to rate how often they are bothered by general health issues (e.g., "*Cold*") ranging from 1 "*Not bothered*" to 4 "*Greatly bothered*". The PIM has shown adequate internal consistency in this sample ($\alpha = 0.78$).

Data Analysis

Descriptive statistics were generated for the continuous variables (life satisfaction, physical illness, mental distress, Facebook-based social support, time spent on Facebook, number of Facebook Friends, and age), and categorical variables (gender). Correlations between the variables were also examined. A structural equation model (SEM) was used to examine the first three hypotheses (H1, H2a, H2b, and H3). The model consisted of 6 observed variables: stress, time spent on Facebook, number of Facebook Friends, Facebook-based social support, with age and gender being included as controls. Physical and mental health concerns were expressed as a latent variable, with 3 observed variables: mental distress, physical illness, and dissatisfaction with life. To test model fit χ^2, comparative fit index (CFI), Tucker-Lewis index (TLI), and root-mean square error of approximation (RMSEA) were used (Kline, 2011). Acceptable fit to the data was indicated by CFI and TLI values of ≥ 0.90, with values of ≥ 0.95 indicating excellent fit. Additionally, RMSEA values of ≥ 0.06 but ≤ 0.08 indicated acceptable fit, with values of < 0.06 indicating excellent fit (Kline, 2011). To test the fourth hypothesis (H4), a multi-group analysis of the model was also conducted to test if the effects of Facebook-based social support was consistent across both groups (metropolitan and regional Facebook users).

RESULTS

Data screening was conducted in IBM SPSS version 24. Additionally, independent samples t-tests showed that the metropolitan sample reported lower levels of mental distress ($t = -2.42$, $p = 0.016$, $d = 0.25$), and higher levels of Facebook-based social support ($t = 1.97$, $p = 0.050$, $d = 0.15$) than the regional sample. No other differences were detected in any of the other variables. The structural equation models (SEMs) were designed and tested in IBM SPSS AMOS version 24. Modification indices showed that age negatively co-varied with perceived life stress and number of Facebook friends. See Table 2 for variable correlations.

The resulting model (see Fig. 1) showed an acceptable-to-strong fit to the data: $\chi^2(23) = 61.58$, CFI $= 0.95$, TLI $= 0.92$, RMSEA $= 0.068$. As predicted, the number of Facebook Friends was positively associated with Facebook-based social support ($\beta = 0.30$, $p < 0.001$), however,

Table 2 Correlations, means, and standard deviations of the variables in the structural equation model ($N = 367$)

	1	2	3	4	5	6	7	8	9	10
1. Gender	–									
2. Age	−0.03	–								
3. Perceived stress	−0.01	−0.26	–							
4. Number of Facebook friends	0.13*	−0.41	0.07	–						
5. Time spent on Facebook (Hours)	−0.01	−0.13*	0.14**	0.15**	–					
6. Facebook-based social support	0.10	−0.12*	−0.25	0.35**	0.13*	–				
7. Health (composite)	−0.05	−0.20	0.79***	0.03	0.18**	−0.25	–			
8. Physical illness	0.14**	−0.15**	0.47***	0.04	0.12*	−0.13*	0.69***	–		
9. Mental distress	−0.11*	−0.20	0.75***	0.06	0.17**	−0.21	0.91***	0.47***	–	
10. Dissatisfaction with life	−0.06	−0.10	0.59***	−0.06	0.13*	−0.25	0.73***	0.34***	0.49***	–
M	–	36.30	28.43	341.92	1.56	32.83	64.00	15.71	37.18	11.12
SD	–	12.95	7.00	377.99	1.60	7.91	20.48	5.99	12.43	6.87

*$p < 0.05$, **$p < 0.01$, ***$p < 0.001$

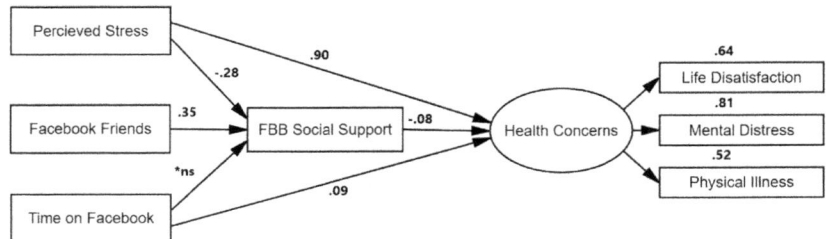

Fig. 1 The effect of Facebook-based social support on physical and mental health concerns (*Note* *ns = non-significant, FBB = Facebook-based. For ease of interpretation control variables, error terms, and covariances are not shown)

time spent on Facebook was not significantly associated with Facebook-based social support ($\beta = 0.09$, $p = 0.05$), resulting in partial support for H1. Additionally, increased perceived life stress and time spent on Facebook were both significantly associated with greater physical and mental health concerns ($\beta = 0.90$, $p < 0.001$; $\beta = 0.09$, $p = 0.015$, respectively), providing support for H2a and H2b. Finally, increased Facebook-based social support was found to reduce levels of physical and mental health concerns ($\beta = -0.08$, $p = 0.050$), and mediate the indirect relationship between perceived life stress, and physical and mental health concerns ($\beta = 0.02$, $p = 0.040$). This finding supports the hypothesis that Facebook-based social support can reduce the effect of perceived life stress on physical and mental health concerns (H3). Age and gender were not significantly associated with physical and mental health concerns ($\beta = 0.01$, $p = 0.92$; $\beta = 0.06$, $p = 0.09$, respectively).

THE ROLE OF LOCATION ON FACEBOOK-BASED SOCIAL SUPPORT

To test the role of location on Facebook-based social support, a multi-group analysis was also conducted, with the location of the user (metropolitan and regional users) as the grouping variable. The model showed strong fit to the data: $\chi^2(46) = 77.36$, CFI = 0.96, TLI = 0.94, RMSEA = 0.043. Additionally, the unconstrained model significantly differed from the constrained model ($p = 0.036$), suggesting that the location of the user was a significant moderator of the hypothesised model. Within the metropolitan sample (Fig. 2), greater levels of Facebook-based social support were associated with lower levels of physical and mental health concerns ($\beta = -0.13$, $p = 0.016$). Interestingly, time spent on Facebook was not significantly associated with either Facebook-based social support, or physical and mental health concerns ($\beta = 0.07$, $p = 0.25$; $\beta = 0.01$, $p = 0.83$, respectively). Additionally, Facebook-based social support did mediate the effects of increased perceived life stress on physical and mental health concerns ($\beta = 0.03$, $p = 0.010$).

Within the regional sample (Fig. 3), Facebook-based social support was not associated with physical and mental health concerns ($\beta = -0.02$, $p = 0.69$), showing that Facebook-based social support does not mediate

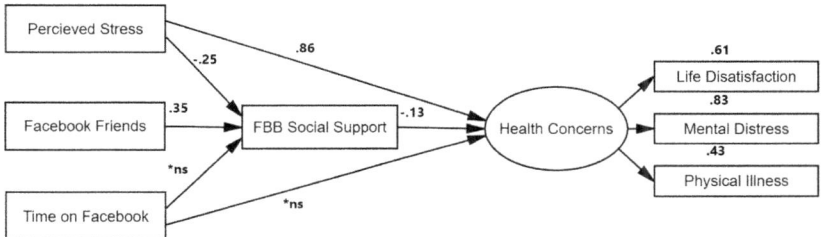

Fig. 2 The effect of Facebook-based social support on physical and mental health concerns in the metropolitan sample (*Note* *ns = non-significant, FBB = Facebook-based. For ease of interpretation control variables, error terms, and covariances are not shown)

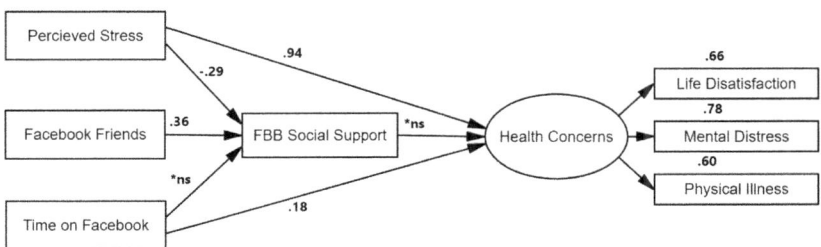

Fig. 3 The effect of Facebook-based social support on physical and mental health concerns in the regional sample (*Note* *ns = non-significant, FBB = Facebook-based. For ease of interpretation control variables, error terms, and covariances are not shown)

the relationship between perceived life stress, and physical and mental health concerns. This result does not support the hypothesis that the effect of Facebook-based social support on physical and mental health concerns would be strongest for the regional sample (H4). Interestingly, more time spent on Facebook was associated with greater physical and mental health concerns in the regional sample only ($\beta = 0.18$, $p < 0.001$), with the same effect being non-significant in the metropolitan sample.

Discussion

This study aimed to explore the effects of Facebook-based social support on physical and mental health concerns across metropolitan and regional samples. Overall, there was partial support for the hypotheses proposed by this study. H1 was partially supported: greater numbers of Facebook Friends were associated with greater levels of Facebook-based social support, which was consistent with previous studies (Gilmour et al., 2019; Kim & Lee, 2011; Nabi et al., 2013). However, time spent on Facebook was not associated with Facebook-based social support, suggesting that the quality of social interactions could be of greater utility rather than the total time spent on Facebook (Gilmour et al., 2019). Greater perceived life stress was associated with greater physical and mental health concerns (H2a), which was consistent with previous studies examining stress and health (Cohen & Wills, 1985; Thoits, 1986; Zhang, 2017). Interestingly greater time spent on Facebook, previously associated with poorer health outcomes (Frost & Rickwood, 2017), was only significantly associated with greater physical and mental health concerns in the regional sample (H2b). Within the total sample, increased Facebook-based social support did mediate the relationship between increased life stress and greater physical and mental health concerns (H3). However, while Facebook-based social support in the metropolitan sample was significantly associated with lower levels of physical and mental health concerns, within the regional sample this relationship was not supported.

The overall findings of this study showed that in the regional sample, Facebook-based social support did not affect physical and mental health concerns. This result runs counter to the fourth hypothesis (H4) and there are several possible explanations for this finding. Firstly, Facebook-based social support has been found to be largely redundant in persons with high levels of face-to-face social support (Cole et al., 2017), and can be utilised when opportunities for face-to-face interactions are reduced

(Indian & Grieve, 2014). Thus, contrary to previous literature, it may be that individuals who live in regional communities may have sufficient face-to-face support and require less Facebook-based support. Additionally, it may be that regional Facebook user have different motivations for using Facebook, beyond the need to belong and maintain relationships (Nadkarni & Hofmann, 2012). The regional sample also reported lower levels of Facebook-based social support when compared to the metropolitan sample.

Interestingly, the regional sample reported significantly higher numbers of Facebook Friends, previously found to have a negative impact on physical and mental health when online social networks are large and complex (Campisi et al., 2012, 2017; Gilmour et al., 2019; Kim & Lee, 2011). Additionally, access to both mobile and fixed internet services in regional Australian areas can be more problematic than in metropolitan areas (Park, 2017), possibly contributing to making Facebook-based social support difficult or challenging for regional Facebook users. This result also suggests Facebook-based social support may only have a positive effect on health outcomes within metropolitan communities, as previous studies that examine the effects of Facebook-based social support on health have mostly drawn entirely on undergraduate or metropolitan-based samples (Gilmour et al., 2019).

Increased time spent on Facebook was associated with greater levels of health concerns in the regional sample. Accessing internet-based activities, like Facebook, have been found to promote sedentary behaviour, resulting in reduced physical health activities, like exercise, and has been associated with greater levels of depression (Barkley & Lepp, 2016; Frost & Rickwood, 2017). As individuals living in regional areas are less likely to engage in positive health activities (AIHW, 2016, 2019), the time spent on Facebook could impact the likelihood of individuals engaging in positive health activities.

Limitations and Future Research

There are a few limitations to this study. First, this study is cross-sectional, making causal inferences difficult. Second, it has been found that strong and weak social ties on Facebook, as well as communication competence, can affect Facebook-based social support and health outcomes (Kim, 2014; Wright et al., 2013). This study did not control for how strong or weak interpersonal ties and communication competence can affect

Facebook-based social support. Reviewing the strength of social ties on Facebook, across metropolitan and regional samples, could demonstrate a difference in the structure of a person's Facebook network, and could present options for future research. Additionally, as there is a disparity in internet access and speed across Australian communities (Park, 2017) this may have played a role in using Facebook as a mechanism for social support, which could have presented a control needed for this study. However, given that regional-based participants reported greater numbers of Facebook Friends and time spent on Facebook, it is possible that this disparity in internet access may not have impacted this study. Finally, while the metropolitan and regional samples were separated using the ASGS Remoteness Areas criteria (ABS, 2016; AIHW, 2004), an investigation into Australians living in extremely remote conditions was not captured in the recruitment of this study and could require future research.

CONCLUSION

This chapter aimed to examine the effects of Facebook-based social support on physical and mental health concerns, such as mental distress, dissatisfaction with life, and physical illness, across regional and metropolitan samples, key areas of focus for both developmental and social psychologists. Facebook-based social support was associated with lower levels of physical and mental health concerns in the metropolitan sample. However, within the regional sample, Facebook-based social support did not buffer individuals from increased perceived life stress, and greater time spent on Facebook was associated with greater physical and mental health concerns. Overall, our findings have shown that the effects of social support drawn from Facebook on health could be location-specific, and when examining technology engagement and use environmental factors need to be considered when examining the impacts on individuals and their development.

REFERENCES

ABS. (2016). *Australian Statistical Geography Standard (ASGS): Volume 5 – Remoteness Structure.* http://www.abs.gov.au/AUSSTATS/abs@.nsf/Latest products/1270.0.55.005Main%20Features15July%202016?opendocument& tabname=Summary&prodno=1270.0.55.005&issue=July%202016&num=& view=. Retrieved from March 26, 2020.

AIHW. (2004). Rural, regional and remote health: A guide to remoteness classifications. *Canberra: Australian Institute of Health and Welfare AIHW Cat. No. PHE, 53*. https://www.aihw.gov.au/. Retrieved from January 1, 2020.

AIHW. (2016). *Australia's Health 2016: 5.11 Rural and remote health*. http://www.aihw.gov.au/australias-health/2016/population-groups/#t12. Retrieved from January 1, 2020.

AIHW. (2019). *Rural & remote health*. https://www.aihw.gov.au/reports/rural-remote-australians/rural-remote-health/contents/summary. Retrieved from January 1, 2020.

Alston, M. (2012). Rural male suicide in Australia. *Social Science & Medicine, 74*(4), 515–522. https://doi.org/10.1016/j.socscimed.2010.04.036

Barkley, J. E., & Lepp, A. (2016). Mobile phone use among college students is a sedentary leisure behavior which may interfere with exercise. *Computers in Human Behavior, 56*, 29–33. https://doi.org/10.1016/j.chb.2015.11.001

Bourke, L., Humphreys, J. S., Wakerman, J., & Taylor, J. (2012). Understanding rural and remote health: A framework for analysis in Australia. *Health & Place, 18*(3), 496–503. https://doi.org/10.1016/j.healthplace.2012.02.009

Campbell, P., Wynne-Jones, G., & Dunn, K. M. (2011). The influence of informal social support on risk and prognosis in spinal pain: A systematic review. *European Journal of Pain, 15*(5), 444. e441–444.e414. https://doi.org/10.1016/j.ejpain.2010.09.011

Campisi, J., Bynog, P., McGehee, H., Oakland, J. C., Quirk, S., Taga, C., & Taylor, M. (2012). Facebook, stress, and incidence of upper respiratory infection in undergraduate college students. *Cyberpsychology, Behavior, and Social Networking, 15*(12), 675–681. https://doi.org/10.1089/cyber.2012.0156

Campisi, J., May, J., Burch, K., Larson, K., Doscher, J., Doherty, S., Isaacson, K., Sebring, K., & Gahan, A. (2017). Anxiety-inducing Facebook behavior is associated with higher rates of upper respiratory infection in college-aged users [Article]. *Computers in Human Behavior, 76*, 211–217. https://doi.org/10.1016/j.chb.2017.07.022

Cohen, S., Kamarck, T., & Mermelstein, R. (1983). A global measure of perceived stress. *Journal of Health and Social Behavior*, 385–396. https://doi.org/10.2307/2136404

Cohen, S., & Wills, T. A. (1985). Stress, social support, and the buffering hypothesis. *Psychological Bulletin, 98*(2), 310. https://doi.org/10.1037/0033-2909.98.2.310

Cole, D. A., Nick, E. A., Zelkowitz, R. L., Roeder, K. M., & Spinelli, T. (2017). Online social support for young people: Does it recapitulate in-person social support; can it help? *Computers in Human Behavior, 68*, 456–464. https://doi.org/10.1016/j.chb.2016.11.058

Crowling, D. (2016). *Social Media Statistics - June 2016*. www.socialmedianews.com.au. Retrieved from March 29, 2020.

Diener, E., Emmons, R. A., Larsen, R. J., & Griffin, S. (1985). The satisfaction with life scale. *Journal of Personality Assessment, 49*(1), 71–75.

Fraser, C., Judd, F., Jackson, H., Murray, G., Humphreys, J., & Hodgins, G. A. (2002). Does one size really fit all? Why the mental health of rural Australians requires further research. *Australian Journal of Rural Health, 10*(6), 288–295.

Frost, R. L., & Rickwood, D. J. (2017). A systematic review of the mental health outcomes associated with Facebook use. *Computers in Human Behavior, 76*, 576–600. https://doi.org/10.1016/j.chb.2017.08.001

Gilmour, J., Machin, T., Brownlow, C., & Jeffries, C. (2019). Facebook-based social support and health: A systematic review. *Psychology of Popular Media Culture*, No Pagination Specified-No Pagination Specified. https://doi.org/10.1037/ppm0000246

Henry, J. D., & Crawford, J. R. (2005). The short-form version of the Depression Anxiety Stress Scales (DASS-21): Construct validity and normative data in a large non-clinical sample. *British Journal of Clinical Psychology, 44*(2), 227–239.

Hewitt, P. L., Flett, G. L., & Mosher, S. W. (1992). The Perceived Stress Scale: Factor structure and relation to depression symptoms in a psychiatric sample. *Journal of Psychopathology and Behavioral Assessment, 14*(3), 247–257.

Indian, M., & Grieve, R. (2014). When Facebook is easier than face-to-face: Social support derived from Facebook in socially anxious individuals. *Personality and Individual Differences, 59*, 102–106. https://doi.org/10.1016/j.paid.2013.11.016

Jackson, B., Sellers, R. M., & Peterson, C. (2002). Pessimistic explanatory style moderates the effect of stress on physical illness. *Personality and Individual Differences, 32*(3), 567–573. https://doi.org/10.1016/S0191-8869(01)00061-7

Kawachi, I., & Berkman, L. F. (2001). Social ties and mental health. *Journal of Urban Health: Bulletin of the New York Academy of Medicine, 78*(3), 458–467. https://doi.org/10.1093/jurban/78.3.458

Kelly, B. J., Stain, H. J., Coleman, C., Perkins, D., Fragar, L., Fuller, J., Lewin, T. J., Lyle, D., Carr, V. J., & Wilson, J. M. (2010). Mental health and well-being within rural communities: The Australian Rural Mental Health Study. *Australian Journal of Rural Health, 18*(1), 16–24. https://doi.org/10.1111/j.1440-1584.2009.01118.x

Kim, H. (2014). Enacted social support on social media and subjective well-being. *International Journal of Communication, 8*(1), 2201–2221. https://www.scopus.com/inward/record.uri?eid=2-s2.0-85011600852&partnerID=40&md5=61f62a33d57350e3111c5133f026c8d4. Retrieved from January 21, 2020.

Kim, J., & Lee, J.-E.R. (2011). The Facebook paths to happiness: Effects of the number of Facebook friends and self-presentation on subjective well-being. *Cyberpsychology, Behavior, and Social Networking, 14*(6), 359–364. https://doi.org/10.1089/cyber.2010.0374

Kline, R. B. (2011). *Principles and practice of structural equation modeling* (3rd ed.). Guilford Publications.

Koopman, C., Angell, K., Turner-Cobb, J. M., Kreshka, M. A., Donnelly, P., McCoy, R., Turkseven, A., Graddy, K., Giese-Davis, J., & Spiegel, D. (2001). Distress, coping, and social support among rural women recently diagnosed with primary breast cancer. *The Breast Journal, 7*(1), 25–33. https://doi.org/10.1046/j.1524-4741.2001.007001025.x

Lauckner, H., & Hutchinson, S. (2016). Peer support for people with chronic conditions in rural areas: a scoping review. *Rural & Remote Health, 16*(1). https://doi.org/10.21203/rs.2.16656/v1

Li, X., Chen, W., & Popiel, P. (2015). What happens on Facebook stays on Facebook? The implications of Facebook interaction for perceived, receiving, and giving social support. *Computers in Human Behavior, 51*(PA), 106–113. https://doi.org/10.1016/j.chb.2015.04.066

Luszczynska, A., Pawlowska, I., Cieslak, R., Knoll, N., & Scholz, U. (2013). Social support and quality of life among lung cancer patients: A systematic review. *Psycho-Oncology, 22*(10), 2160–2168. https://doi.org/10.1002/pon.3218

Nabi, R. L., Prestin, A., & So, J. (2013). Facebook friends with (health) benefits? Exploring social network site use and perceptions of social support, stress, and well-being. *Cyberpsychology, Behavior, and Social Networking, 16*(10), 721–727. https://doi.org/10.1089/cyber.2012.0521

Nadkarni, A., & Hofmann, S. G. (2012). Why do people use Facebook? *Personality and Individual Differences, 52*(3), 243–249. https://doi.org/10.1016/j.paid.2011.11.007

Osman, A., Wong, J. L., Bagge, C. L., Freedenthal, S., Gutierrez, P. M., & Lozano, G. (2012). The depression anxiety stress Scales—21 (DASS-21): Further examination of dimensions, scale reliability, and correlates. *Journal of Clinical Psychology, 68*(12), 1322–1338. https://doi.org/10.1002/jclp.21908

Park, S. (2017). Digital inequalities in rural Australia: A double jeopardy of remoteness and social exclusion. *Journal of Rural Studies, 54*, 399–407. https://doi.org/10.1016/j.jrurstud.2015.12.018

Pavot, W., & Diener, E. (1993). Review of the satisfaction with life scale. *Psychological Assessment, 5*(2), 164. https://doi.org/10.1037/1040-3590.5.2.164

Pavot, W., & Diener, E. (2008). The satisfaction with life scale and the emerging construct of life satisfaction. *The Journal of Positive Psychology, 3*(2), 137–152. https://doi.org/10.1080/17439760701756946

Sapolsky, R. M. (1994). *Why zebras don't get ulcers*. WH Freeman New York.

Sensis. (2017). *Sensis Social Media Report: Chapter 1 – Australians and social media*. Sensis. www.sensis.com.au/socialmediareport. Retrieved from March 16, 2020.

Statistica. (2020). *Number of social network users worldwide from 2010 to 2021*. Statistica. https://www.statista.com/statistics/278414/number-of-worldwide-social-network-users/. Retrieved from January 27, 2020.

Thoits, P. A. (1986). Social support as coping assistance. *Journal of Consulting and Clinical Psychology, 54*(4), 416. https://doi.org/10.1037/0022-006x.54.4.416

Vyavaharkar, M., Moneyham, L., Corwin, S., Saunders, R., Annang, L., & Tavakoli, A. (2010). Relationships between stigma, social support, and depression in HIV-infected African American women living in the rural Southeastern United States. *Journal of the Association of Nurses in AIDS Care, 21*(2), 144–152. https://doi.org/10.1016/j.jana.2009.07.008

Wallston, B. S., Alagna, S. W., DeVellis, B. M., & DeVellis, R. F. (1983). Social support and physical health. *Health Psychology, 2*(4), 367.

Wright, K. B. (2012). Emotional Support and Perceived Stress Among College Students Using Facebook.com: An Exploration of the Relationship Between Source Perceptions and Emotional Support. *Communication Research Reports, 29*(3), 175–184. https://doi.org/10.1080/08824096.2012.695957

Wright, K. B., Rosenberg, J., Egbert, N., Ploeger, N. A., Bernard, D. R., & King, S. (2013). Communication competence, social support, and depression among college students: A model of Facebook and face-to-face support network influence. *Journal of Health Communication, 18*(1), 41–57. https://doi.org/10.1080/10810730.2012.688250

Wrigley, S., Jackson, H., Judd, F., & Komiti, A. (2005). Role of stigma and attitudes toward help-seeking from a general practitioner for mental health problems in a rural town. *Australian and New Zealand Journal of Psychiatry, 39*(6), 514–521. https://doi.org/10.1111/j.1440-1614.2005.01612.x

Zhang, R. (2017). The stress-buffering effect of self-disclosure on Facebook: An examination of stressful life events, social support, and mental health among college students. *Computers in Human Behavior, 75*, 527–537. https://doi.org/10.1016/j.chb.2017.05.043

What Grief isn't: Dead Grief Concepts and Their Digital-Age Revival

Mórna O'Connor and Elaine Kasket

Abstract We used to think grief was about moving through a set of prescribed stages, a process after which we would be 'over it' and resume normality. However, this view has been dismissed, and the deleterious effects of such universal, linear, and reductive grief accounts are well established. Multi-disciplinary theory and research suggest there's no right, one or healthy way to grieve; no stages, steps, or prescriptions. Rather, grief involves survivors telling stories of their dead, their relationship to them, and themselves, in relationships with others doing the same, these stories shaped by societies and cultures. Within these shifting parameters, our stories of our dead are interpretive, creative, and active, and our griefs are as idiosyncratic and diverse as the relationships to which they pertain. However, with the digitalisation of life over the last two decades, old ideas about grief have crept back in. In this chapter, we show

M. O'Connor (✉)
University of Nottingham, Nottingham, UK
e-mail: morna.oconnor@nottingham.ac.uk

E. Kasket
University of Wolverhampton, Wolverhampton, UK

how, at the intersection of grief and the digital, three long-debunked notions about grief are reviving: (i) that there's a normal way to grieve, (ii) that technology helps or hinders grief, and (iii) that we must control technology's impact on the bereaved. We use longitudinal, qualitative data to problematise the digital-age reanimation of these dead grief concepts, and to illustrate their continued inappropriateness for contemporary grievers.

Keywords Technology · Grief · Digital · Online · Grief stages · Dead grief concepts · Grief norms · Bereavement · Mourning

What is Grief? Assumptions Old and New

Even before we experience it ourselves, we carry ideas about grief. Our assumptions about grieving are shaped by multiple forces: stories, films, television, and the experiences of others. Local customs and traditions of ritual and expression dictate how grief is done 'around here'. After experiencing a significant loss ourselves, we may believe we've learnt what grief 'is'.

From the early 1900s, the new science of psychology instructed us on what to expect following loss. From Freud (1917) onwards, Western psychology and psychiatry opined on grief without systematically studying it, and their theories about 'normal' grieving were accepted as conventional wisdom (Klass & Steffen, 2018). Stage models, describing grief as a series of steps ending in 'letting go' or 'moving on' (e.g., Kübler-Ross, 1970; Worden, 1982), and heavily influenced by medical frameworks of healing and cure, persisted for close to 100 years.

For every person comforted by a series of predictable steps culminating in release from sadness, another compares themselves against these stages and believes they are 'doing grief wrong'. As this century dawned, however, a new generation of bereavement research challenged the belief that grief follows a predictable course. Books like *Continuing Bonds: New Understandings of Grief* (Klass et al., 1996) presented empirical, multidisciplinary, longitudinal evidence of the idiosyncrasy of grief, demonstrating that it is interpretive and steeped in context. Linear movement through grief stages was exposed for what it is: a myth.

Before the new ideas about grief in *Continuing Bonds* could trickle through to the popular imagination, however, the world's information landscape changed dramatically. Try entering 'grief' into a search engine. What messages about grief do you get from the links to which you're directed, the blurbs that appear under results, and the list of questions posed by other searchers? Believe what the algorithms deliver, and you'll be convinced that grief does indeed happen in a succession of stages; that some grief experiences are normal, and others are not.

Why, despite the ample research debunking 'normal' grief, are we still so in sway to the idea? Several factors may play a role. First, when we are anxious, we tend to double down on familiar knowledge, simple answers, and the twin comforts of prediction and control (Hayes et al., 2016). Perhaps we find solace in the simplicity of a stage model's promise: orderly, time-bound progress through and beyond grief. Second, the ways we use technologies in grieving are not neutral but framed by developers who incorporate their own beliefs about grieving into platforms and services. The success of any business relies upon accurate predictions about the market, and companies who deal in death and the digital try to predict what will be useful to, healthy for, or desired by bereaved users. Finally, as you will have seen if you carried out the search-engine experiment, our algorithmic environment reinstates and reinforces people's existing beliefs about grief, irrespective of their truth value.

In this chapter, we examine three persistent grief assumptions that we argue are finding new life in the modern digital environment: First, that there is an ideal way to grieve; second, that technology helps or hinders grieving; and third, that we must control technology's impact on the bereaved. The continued dominance of these assumptions is evident not just to those who consume or undertake formal research in this field, but is observable in discourse about grief on and offline, in the very architecture of the digital space, and in the terms and conditions that regulate it. Once orientated to them, you will hear them in how people speak and react to one another about grief, spot them in news stories, pick them up in online comments and information, and find them embedded in digital platforms and designs. In the following sections, we use research data and anecdotal illustrations from contemporary media and scholarly literature to evidence these assumptions, employing empirically supported theories to problematise them, and suggest alternative understandings.

Assumption 1: 'There's a Normal Way to Grieve'

The first dead grief concept reviving in the digital age is that there are right and wrong ways to grieve. We assume there is a normal process, a healthier way, a predictable series of phases or emotional experiences through which grievers should travel. The death of such 'grief norms' is well established in academic literature. '[W]hen we look...at the emotional experiences of bereaved people over time', says psychologist and grief researcher George Bonanno (2010), 'the level of fluctuation is nothing short of spectacular' (p. 41). Online, though, the idea of normal grieving lives on. In this section we briefly illustrate three ways that notions of normal grieving are promulgated in the digital environment.

First, well-known organisations, health services, and providers still foreground stage models and other 'norm' frameworks in their online resources. For example, the bereavement guidance on the UK's National Health Service (NHS) website states that bereaved people may have a range of experiences; however, they then list 'common symptoms' and outline four stages of grief, which, they claim, 'experts generally accept' (NHS, 2019). Another popular source of information for the British public, the mental-health charity Mind, also briefly acknowledges the variety in people's grief experiences. Far more text, however, is devoted to describing the famous 'stages of grief' (Mind UK, 2019). Elizabeth Kübler-Ross used these stages to describe the experiences of *dying* people, not those mourning them, but they were subsequently transplanted and applied to mourning, becoming reified as 'the' grief stages: denial, anger, bargaining, depression, and acceptance (Kübler-Ross, 1970). Where you're searching from matters for the message you receive. In contrast to the UK, the downloadable fact sheets from the Australian Centre for Grief and Bereavement (2019) contain no reference to stages, symptoms, normal reactions, or common responses, emphasising instead the idiosyncrasy of the grief experience. In a climate where reliable and valid information can be hard to identify, it's positive when official sources head up the results of an online search. However, such sources can spread outmoded, unhelpfully prescriptive ideas about grief, reinforcing their credibility and maintaining their influence.

Second, grief norms are alive and well online, as cultures of mourning from across the globe meet, mix, and clash. Online communities commonly engage in 'grief policing' (Gach et al., 2017): attempts to reorientate others to supposed norms about how grief 'should' look, act, and feel. In 2016, waves of grief on social media for Prince, David Bowie, and Alan Rickman were met by vicious criticism for mourning a celebrity (Long, 2016), questioning grief's idiosyncratic nature and causing grievers to doubt the normality or acceptability of their feelings. Grievers are commonly challenged on sites like Twitter, which were not developed as mourning or remembrance platforms, but optimised for debate and strong, often polarised, public discourse. Grief policing is not restricted to any one platform or death type, however, and is readily apparent in comment threads as people enact rules and biases about grief. These rules and biases rest on the notion that there's a normal grief response, and rail against deviations from that supposed norm.

Finally, devices and online platforms used heavily during life ultimately become containers for dead people's data. Social media, email, and cloud account providers have become powerful actors in the modern grieving landscape, with the authority to grant or deny the bereaved access to sentimental and practical information relating to their dead. News stories lament the tragedy of grievers beseeching technology companies to grant or restore access to their loved ones' personal information and devices, and condemning their cold denial of what these survivors so desperately need (e.g. Marchitelli, 2020). The assumption is clear: grievers desire access to material related to their dead, and parties denying this block ideal grieving. Some grief experts frame denial or loss of access as a 'second loss', suggesting that mourners 'live in fear of losing' such digital material (Bassett, 2019a).

The experiences of many bereaved interviewees in Mórna O'Connor's (2020) doctoral research challenged this new, digital-age grief norm. Conducting multiple successive interviews with clusters of individuals grieving the loss of the same person, Mórna found that the idiosyncrasy, fluidity, and unpredictability of grief holds true with digital material. For some of her participants, maintaining access was indeed critically important at times; however, others' experiences challenged the popular assumption that access to digital material is always important, especially amongst 'inner circle' bereaved.

One participant, 'Brian', had lost his wife 'Deborah'. The couple had shared a love of travel and also a desktop computer, which housed a lifetime of photographs from their adventures together, as well as many other personal and professional files related to their intertwined lives. Unlike many grievers interviewed by the media, Brian did not need to go head-to-head with Apple or Facebook for access to this material related to Deborah—it was his if he wanted it.

At the time of his first interview with Mórna, Deborah had been dead for about three years. The importance Brian placed on this wealth of digital material, though, was related to not looking at it, but having the open-ended *potential* to do so. For him, the value of the material grew over time, like an unopened bottle of fine wine.

> *As time goes on, it perhaps builds up even more. A specialness, you want to consider those things really, take time over sorting them out....To know there's something there to look at, physical evidence still there really, also you do perhaps build it up into this sacred act, which is a bit silly probably, this sacred act of reverence: the treasured artefacts.* ('Brian', first interview)

Five months later, Brian still hadn't looked at the material on the shared computer, and his way of experiencing the material—as with so many other Mórna's research participants—had shifted with time. Like the anticipation of a longed-for gift, Brian took comfort in imagining all the surprises and joys the material might contain if he delved into it. Imagining the material felt rich with possibility.

> *the same for the digital files [on the shared desktop], so there still is a comfort in having them there, to think there might be little gems and things I want to save...wherever there's something else to look through, there's still an element of her around. If I took a week and went through it all that would be it...I might feel it was all behind me.* ('Brian', second interview)

When so much of the popular discourse suggests that 'normal' grieving involves desiring access to digital material relating to our dead, we place expectations on people to grieve to a template and call into question experiences like Brian's. For Brian, access was not the goal; not accessing material made space for him to imagine and anticipate. Having something yet to look through was a comfort that made Brian feel something of Deborah was still around.

Assumption 2: 'Technology Helps or Hinders Grief'

The second dead grief concept finding new life in the digital environment is that grief can be helped or hindered by outside forces. Today, technology is this make-or-break force, either enabling us to grieve better or disrupting how grief 'should' be. Although the force here is new, questions about its positive or negative impact on grief are old. Dennis Klass, co-author of *Continuing Bonds*, refers to the strength and recurrence of this 'help or hinder' reflex in grief scholarship (Klass, 2006). Klass warns his fellow grief researchers of this 'causality trap' (p. 847), where the force in question 'helps or hinders healthy coping, good adjustment, and so on' (p. 844) and therefore relies on the idea that there's a normal way to grieve. As with the last assumption, several factors are involved in reworking old causal help-or-hinder assumptions for a new digital age.

First, as Jacobsen (2020) noted, 'death is now visible within many different quarters of the academic world as a topic of intense research interest' (p. 12). Grief specialists are not the only observers focused on death and mourning in a digital context. Philosophers, anthropologists, sociologists, media scholars, computer–human interaction (CHI) specialists, legal scholars, and tech entrepreneurs make up this multidisciplinary community and old grief assumptions are creeping back in.

The 'help or hinder' discourse is present in the earliest work on death, grief, and the digital. In the influential edited text *Dying, Death, and Grief in an Online Universe* (Sofka et al., 2012), the view that technology has negative implications for grief is so pronounced that its foreword remarked upon the volume's frequent use of the term *brave new world*, with its 'sense of foreboding of the dystopia Huxley once described' (Doka, 2012, p. xii). Another widely cited article in the field, '*Does the Internet change how we die and mourn?*' (Walter et al., 2011) describes 'online practices that *may affect* dying, the funeral, grief and memorialization, inheritance and archaeology' (our emphasis, p. 275). While these authors do not suggest negative impact, they imply that technology has the potential to change grief from what it would otherwise be.

A causal, help-or-hinder flavour flows through much contemporary research about death and technology (e.g., Baglione et al., 2018; Bassett, 2015, 2018, 2019b; Braman et al., 2011). On the 'help' side, Braman et al. (2011) suggest that 'Passing on technological artifacts from our lives or digital objects, can be helpful for those trying to overcome loss'

(p. 187). On the 'hinder' side, Bassett warns of the 'ramifications of data loss and access restriction' for those grieving (2020, p. 84). In a chapter published almost a decade after *Dying, Death, and Grief in an Online Universe*, Sofka (2020) again invoked this help-or-hinder duality, asking 'Does the presence of a Digital Afterlife have a positive or negative impact on survivors' process of coping with grief?' (p. 62).

Second, online news media and journalism persistently frame digital-age grief in simple 'good or bad' terms, as illustrated in the following approaches made to Elaine and Mórna from international media outlets.

> *The Face, London*: 'I'm looking to speak to a specialist in bereavement about how helpful these [digital] tools are when dealing with bereavement.'
> **BBC TV News**: 'It seems a good opportunity to look at the topical issue of digital legacy and we'd love to include your thoughts about the impact this can cause.'
> **BBC Radio 4**: 'We're looking into a story today relating to how technology affects the grieving process.'
> **Vox Media, New York**: 'During my research I came across your excellent work on what happens to our data when we die, how we as a society deal with death online, and the ways in which things like social media have changed the way we mourn.'

Taking for granted that technology affects grief, these journalists wish to pin down exactly *how* grief is being impacted. The dynamics of the modern informational environment play an important part here. Content providers gravitate towards simple ideas and reductive sound bites, consumers expect easily digested information, and some experts give journalists the easy, black-and-white responses they expect. More nuanced accounts run long or don't satisfy the urge for hard-and-fast answers, and grief's complexity can end up on the cutting-room floor.

The first and second dead grief concepts reinforce one another as we conflate normal with good, unusual with bad, old with safety, and new with the danger or excitement of the unknown. As prevalent as digital technology now is, it's a novel force in the grief landscape, depicted as an interloper yet to reveal its true colours: friend or foe?

If easy assumptions start to fall apart at the acknowledgement that there is no defined 'grief' per se, and no predictable impact from any of the disparate phenomena we lump under the category of 'technology', they disintegrate even further at the realisation that *no* element of this system is fixed, stable, or reducible: technology, grief, or any reciprocal impact between the two; griever, grieved, or the relationship between them. In the example below from Mórna's doctoral research (O'Connor, 2020), we unpack this fluidity.

Two years before 'Adam' died, his daughter 'Bella' told her mother a secret she'd discovered: Adam had an affair. Following the revelation, Bella's relationship with both parents deteriorated. After Adam's death, Bella returned to nasty emails from her dad, as well as his Facebook posts, travel blog, and YouTube videos.

> *It's a bit like picking at a scab, isn't it? Because it's almost a thing that stops me romanticising my own past with him, because I do have a compulsion to do that...it's a temptation to reconstruct but I'm not a fan of reconstruction.* ('Bella', second interview)

Finding herself clinging to a sepia-toned narrative of her dad and their relationship, Bella re-engaged with select digital material whenever she wanted to remind herself of Adam's difficult character and their fraught relationship. As the only one of Adam's survivors unwilling to posthumously adulate him, Bella at first saw herself as the sole custodian of the 'real' Adam and used digital material as source material to support her version of the man.

At a later interview, however, Bella challenged the idea of a single truth about Adam: each survivor had their own. Having originally viewed her mother's memory of Adam as falsely adulating, over time she came to see it differently.

> *She does know what he was, and it's hard for her. She needs to say he was a gentleman 'cos that leaves her in a better position...Everything is a construction. There's no such thing as...any truth. Everything that we do is constructed, and what we're always trying to do is construct a positive self and social identity for ourselves and how we construct other people around us. That's what we do as humans.* ('Bella', second interview)

As Bella's grief grew to encompass other stories, truths, and constructs of Adam, she no longer needed to turn to digital material as evidence to verify anything. There was no monolithic 'Adam' to verify, only each person's unique relationship with him, each person's evolving grief, and the interaction of their griefs. Bella's relationship to this digital material is not just *about* her, it is about weaving the material into a story that leaves space for her mother's more clement account of Adam, her marriage to him, and herself as his widow.

This example reminds us how social grief is: it is not about grieving our dead (or their digital remains) alone, but involves people in relationships forming stories of their dead that interact and compete, and in this case, a story that enables a continuing mother–daughter relationship.

The fluid, interpretive, and socially-embedded nature of this grief demonstrates just how simplistic it is to frame technology as helping or hindering it. The help-or-hinder notion runs even further aground when we understand grief—and the part of technology in it—as so steeped in changing relationships and contexts that it is fundamentally incompatible with simple and reductive cause-effect framings.

Assumption 3: 'We Must Control technology's Impact on the Bereaved'

The final dead grief concept reanimating in the digital age is that bereaved people must be protected from forces that we can and should control. In the digital-age revival of this assumption, technology is again cast as this impacting force.

In the previous sections, we showed how the first two dead grief concepts connect, one relying on the other: there's a normal way to grieve, which is helped or hindered by technology. The next step in this sequence of assumptions is a call to action: we must *do something* about technology's impact on the bereaved (Fig. 1).

You can spot this final assumption in action in virtually any news story about technology and grief. In situations where grievers are locked out of the accounts, profiles, and devices of their dead, media often lay the blame at the door of tech companies, stating or implying that they should 'do the right thing' and stop the pain they are charged with causing (TVNZ, 2018).

In comments on these news stories, we again see the assumption in motion. The South Korean mother who met her dead daughter's simulation on a TV show reportedly welcomed the experience, but despite this, the watching and reading public felt moved to take a stand on the true impact of technology on her grief (Global News, 2020). Commenters who saw the VR reunion as inherently 'bad' criticised the documentary

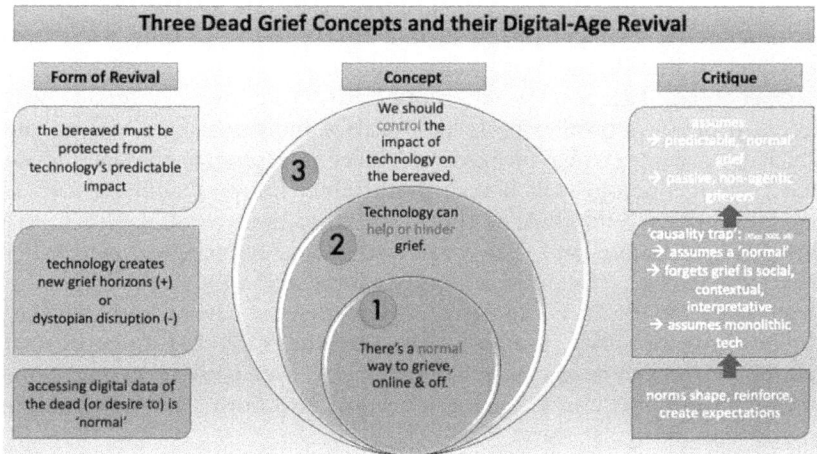

Fig. 1 The three interlocking dead grief concepts, their digital-age revival, and critiques

makers for using this 'cruel' technology to inflict supposed harm on the grieving mother, both explicitly and implicitly asserting that we should not be using technology to 'do this to people'.

Academics direct similar calls to action at tech companies. Arguing that losing data of the dead is a 'second loss' for the bereaved, sociologist Bassett (2018) hopes service providers and designers will take steps to 'mitigate disruption to the bereaved enabled by their platforms' (p. 820). This hope rests on the premise that platforms have the power to disrupt grief and, if certain measures are taken, can remove this disruption.

Technology companies reinforce the idea that they have the power and duty to manage bereaved people's experiences. Since 2007, Facebook has periodically refined its terms and conditions around deceased people's profiles, releasing successive updates to its memorialised-profile design in an effort to get closer to an 'ideal' interface for bereaved users. We see this striving towards optimisation in a Facebook Newsroom headline marking the 2019 changes: 'Making it Easier to Honor a Loved One on Facebook After They Pass Away' (Sandberg, 2019). Multiple changes were made, including the use of AI to identify dead users' profiles *before* they were memorialised. These changes, the news release said, would 'help keep [content] from showing up in places that might *cause distress*, like recommending that person be invited to events or sending a birthday reminder to their friends' (emphasis added).

Over time, Facebook is attempting to make users' interface with deceased people's profiles more bespoke for individual bereaved people, which is laudable. Their messaging, however, promotes the assumption that their technology will have a predictable, universal impact; namely, that automated reminders of the dead cause pain to all grievers, that this pain is negative, and that it can and should be designed out. When they write that they 'hope to minimize experiences that might be painful' (Sandberg, 2019), Facebook situate themselves as having both the duty and power to eliminate pain points that are predictable and universal to all grievers. However, as grief scholars well know, even with good intentions, attempts to predict and harness grief evolve into norms and expectations to grieve in particular ways.

Grief scholars Stroebe and Schut (1999) critique the notions that 'human suffering, integral to grief as we know it, will be considered bad, and that the human condition should only, ideally, encompass positive states and emotions' (p. 203). Under these assumptions, grief is construed as a series of negative steps that must be endured until sadness is resolved or 'closure' found. Evidence suggests, however, that grief is not something fixed that acts on its passive recipients. Grief is formed, made, and constructed by active, interpretive grievers and 'profound beauty can emerge from creativity that is driven by profound loss' (Melnick & Roos, 2007, p. 102). Mórna's research is replete with examples that contradict the model of technology acting predictably upon passive grievers. Instead, her findings show grievers as active narrators, weaving technology into the stories of their grief, of themselves and other survivors, in ways that could not have been designed for or predicted.

For example, after 'Oscar' died, his cousin 'Tina' at first found it distressing to see the record of Oscar's last call, which she'd seen and ignored. She described it as an 'instant negative trigger'.

> *that's probably one of the reasons why I don't go on my [Facebook] messages, because I know that's the first thing that comes up, is like, 'you've missed a call'...I wish I had answered, but I didn't...I'm not going to find out why he called or what he was going to do on that call, but I think that's part of the reason why, because I know that will be an instant negative trigger...the last ever thing is me missing a call.* ('Tina', interview 1)

At an interview three months later, Tina had re-storied the ignored call as just a small component of the cousins' wider relationship. Instead of triggering pain, she now accepted—and even embraced—the record of the missed call as part of 'the rounded…whole thing of our relationship'. Far from passively suffering the predicable impact of the record of Oscar's last call, it was Tina's own creative narration of the call that softened its initial sting. The changing role of the missed call in her grief could not be predicted or designed for, and Tina did not need to be protected from it by, for example, a change in the provider's policies about posthumous retention of missed call records.

Conclusion

These three dead grief concepts too often emerge as answers to three questions: What is grief? What is technology doing to grief? And what should we do about it?

Assumptions persist that we can predict and control grief, that we can and ought to remove pain from grief, and that technology can help accomplish this aim. Perhaps the resurgence and strength of these ideas in the digital age relate to the modern industrial and post-industrial dream that technology will make our lives ever easier, progressively reducing and eliminating friction from our experience. Immersed in this fantasy and in a technologically-infused and controlled environment, grievers are easily constructed as passive agents, to whom both grief and technology happen, and from which they must be protected.

If we are alert to these assumptions, and call them into question when we encounter them, we make space for the infinite diversity of loss experiences and recognise grief as active, agentic, and non-prescribed. The role of grief support is not to shape the narrative for bereaved people—whether that support comes in the form of formal bereavement counselling, input from family, friends and social media contacts, or 'designs for loss' on technology platforms. Rather than resurrecting dead, pre-set stories for grief, many of which come from Western psychological models with limited representation, we should make maximal space for people to shape their own, to include a belief in their own capacity and right to chart their own path through loss. We go awry when we look to technology to be a 'magic bullet', not least because grief need not be seen as an enemy to be shot down.

Each of the three dead grief concepts we have outlined predate the digital age. However, grief concepts die hard, and as we have argued, certain factors at play at this point in history may be causing us to hang on to them that much more tightly. At a time when existing death rituals and traditions are challenged by world events, it is even more important to chip away at unhelpful and inaccurate frameworks in favour of a more compassionate, inclusive understanding of the myriad ways we grieve.

REFERENCES

Australian Centre for Grief and Bereavement (2019). About grief [downloadable resource]. Available on https://www.grief.org.au/ACGB/ACGB_Publications/Resources_for_the_Bereaved/Grief_Information_Sheets.aspx. Accessed 3 May 2020.

Baglione, A. N., Girard, M. M., Price, M., Clawson, J., & Shih, P. C. (2018, April). Modern bereavement: A model for complicated grief in the digital age. *Chi '18: Proceedings of the 2018 CHI Conference on Human Factors in Computing Systems.* Paper No. 416 (1–12). https://doi.org/10.1145/3173574.3173990

Bassett, D. J. (2015). Who wants to live forever? Living, dying and grieving in our digital society. *Social Sciences, 2015*(4), 1127–1139. https://doi.org/10.3390/socsci4041127

Bassett, D. J. (2018). Ctrl + alt + delete: The changing landscape of the uncanny valley and the fear of second loss. *Current Psychology, 40*, 813–821. https://doi.org/10.1007/s12144-018-0006-5

Bassett, D. J. (2019a). Bereaved who take comfort in digital messages from loved ones live in fear of losing them. *The Conversation.* https://theconversation.com/bereaved-who-take-comfort-in-digital-messages-from-dead-loved-ones-live-in-fear-of-losing-them-109754. Accessed 9 April 2022.

Bassett, D. J. (2019b). You only live twice: A constructivist grounded theory study of the creation and inheritance of digital afterlives (Unpublished PhD Thesis). University of Warwick, United Kingdom.

Bassett, D. J. (2020). *Profit and loss: The mortality of the digital immortality platforms. Digital Afterlife: Death Matters in a Digital Age* (pp. 75–88). CRC Press.

Bonanno, G. (2010). *The other side of sadness: What the new science of bereavement tells us about life after loss.* Basic Books.

Braman, J., Dudley, A., & Vincenti, G. (2011). Death, social networks and virtual worlds: A look into the digital afterlife. *Proceedings - 2011 9th International Conference on Software Engineering Research, Management and Applications, SERA 2011.* https://doi.org/10.1109/SERA.2011.35

Doka, K. (2012). Foreword. In C. J. Sofka, I. N. Cupit, and K. Gilbert (Eds.), *Dying, death, and grief in an online universe: For counselors and educators* (pp. xi–xiv). Springer Publishing Company.

Freud, S. (1917 [1915]). *Mourning and melancholia. The standard edition of the complete psychological works of Sigmund Freud, volume XIV (1914–1916): On the history of the psycho-analytic movement, papers on metapsychology and other works* (pp. 237–258). Hogarth Press.

Gach, K., Fiesler, C., & Brubaker, J. (2017). 'Control your emotions, Potter': An analysis of grief policing on Facebook in response to celebrity death. *Proceedings of the ACM on Human-Computer Interaction: Article 47* (pp. 1–18). https://doi.org/10.1145/3134682

Global News. (2020, February 14). Virtual reality 'reunites' mother with dead daughter in South Korean doc. YouTube. https://www.youtube.com/watch?v=0p8HZVCZSkc. Accessed 3 May 2021.

Hayes, S. C., Strosahl, K. D., & Wilson, K. G. (2016). *Acceptance and commitment therapy: The process and practice of mindful change.* Guilford Press.

Jacobsen, M. H. (2020). *The age of spectacular death.* Routledge.

Klass, D. (2006). Continuing conversation about continuing bonds. *Death Studies, 30*, 843–858. https://doi.org/10.1080/07481180600886959

Klass, D., Silverman, P. R., & Nickman, S. L. (Eds.). (1996). *Continuing bonds: New understandings of grief.* Taylor & Francis.

Klass, D., & Steffen, E. M. (2018). Introduction: Continuing bonds—20 years on. In D. Klass, and E. M. Steffen (Eds.), *Series in death, dying, and bereavement. Continuing bonds in bereavement: New directions for research and practice* (pp. 1–14). Routledge/Taylor & Francis Group.

Kübler-Ross, E. (1970). *On death and dying.* Tavistock.

Long, C. (2016, January 17). It's the freakiest show as a lynch mob of Bowie blubberers chases me online. The Sunday Times. https://www.thetimes.co.uk/article/its-the-freakiest-show-as-a-lynch-mob-of-bowie-blubberers-chases-me-online-j73khlxk0sj. Accessed 3 May 2021.

Marchitelli, R. (2020, October 19). Apple blocks widow from honouring husband's dying wish. CBC News. https://www.cbc.ca/news/business/widow-apple-denied-last-words-1.5761926. Accessed 3 May 2021.

Melnick, J., & Roos, S. (2007). The Myth of closure. *Gestalt Review, 11*(2), 90–107.

Mind UK. (2019, July). Bereavement [Web Page]. Retrieved from https://www.mind.org.uk/information-support/guides-to-support-and-services/bereavement/experiences-of-grief/. Accessed 3 May 2021.

NHS (2019, October 15). Grief after bereavement or loss [Web Page]. https://www.nhs.uk/mental-health/feelings-symptoms-behaviours/feelings-and-symptoms/grief-bereavement-loss/. Accessed 15 March 2020.

O'Connor, M. N. (2020). Grief and deceased-related digital culture: An exploratory, longitudinal, qualitative inquiry (Unpublished PhD Thesis). University of Nottingham, United Kingdom.

Sandberg, S. (2019, April 9). Making it easier to honor a loved one on Facebook after they pass away. Facebook Newsroom. https://about.fb.com/news/2019/04/updates-to-memorialization/. Accessed 3 May 2021.

Sofka, C. (2020). The transition from life to the digital afterlife: Thanatechnology and its impact on grief. In M. Savin-Baden & V. Mason-Robbie (Eds.), *Digital afterlife: Death matters in a digital age* (pp. 57–74). CRC Press.

Sofka, C. J., Cupit, I. N., & Gilbert, K. (2012). *Dying, death, and grief in an online universe: For counselors and educators*. Springer Publishing Company.

Stroebe, M., & Schut, H. (1999). The dual process model of coping with bereavement: Rationale and description. *Death Studies, 23*(3), 197–224. https://doi.org/10.1080/074811899201046

TVNZ. (2018, June 11). Grieving widow unable to get photos off dead husband's iPhone, and Apple won't unlock it for her. *YouTube*. https://www.youtube.com/watch?v=UAklZEouL8A. Accessed 3 May 2021.

Walter, T., Hourizi, R., Moncur, W., & Pitsillides, S. (2011). Does the internet change how we die and mourn? Overview and analysis. *Omega, 64*, 275–302. https://doi.org/10.2190/OM.64.4.a

Worden, J. W. (1982). *Grief counselling and grief therapy: A handbook for the mental health practitioner*. New York Springer.

Final Reflections

Charlotte Brownlow, Tanya Machin, Susan Abel, and John Gilmour

Abstract This final chapter of the edited collection seeks to draw together and reflect on the key themes that have been highlighted by the individual chapter authors. The chapters overall highlight the nuanced ways that individuals and groups engage with technology across the lifespan. Overall, three key themes are highlighted for discussion. The first reflects the opportunities for identity exploration and identity management that many of the chapters highlight. The second comprises the positive opportunities afforded by online engagement, which are frequently overlooked in favour of explorations of negative impacts. The third and final overarching theme revisits the engagement with technology throughout the lifespan. While statistics demonstrate differing engagements with online platforms at various life stages, the chapters reflect engagement throughout an individual's life from young childhood through to death. The chapter calls for better understandings as to how technology can enable us to think differently about possibilities

---

C. Brownlow (✉) · T. Machin · S. Abel · J. Gilmour
University of Southern Queensland, Toowoomba, QLD, Australia
e-mail: charlotte.brownlow@usq.edu.au

for connection, support, and the crafting of positive identities, drawing on innovative and dynamic research approaches.

Keywords Social media · Technology · Developmental psychology

In this final chapter we will reflect on some of the key themes that we have identified in bringing together this edited collection. The seven empirical chapters comprising this book are diverse in many ways including the technology or developmental stage of focus and also the methodological approach adopted in their investigation and reflections. What all of the chapters do share however is a common focus on the nuanced ways that we engage with technology and how this is shaping and influencing our lives. The chapters have demonstrated that technology is something that cuts across the entire lifespan, from young children, through negotiating adolescence and online identities, the shaping of working environments and social connections for adults, and finally onto issues of death and bereavement. Previously research has focused heavily on the negative impacts that technology for children and adolescents, especially social media, and what this collection has demonstrated is that childhood and adolescence is just one area of an entire lifespan where individuals engage with technology.

The collection has highlighted three key themes for reflection and informing of potential future research direction: Opportunities for identity exploration and identity management online; Positive possibilities through online engagement; and the engagement with technology across the lifespan. We know from previous literature such as the work of Erik Erikson, that adolescence is a time for individuals to explore their identities and craft these to meet the expectations of both the individual themselves and their peers and broader cultural context. Online groups are therefore a key way for groups of individuals to negotiate identities and maintain social connections. This may be especially important for groups who are marginalised or geographically isolated from like-minded peers. Previously individuals were often limited by geographical boundaries, be these national or international, and online communications offer a range of opportunities for connection with communities that would not have been possible prior to these technological developments. This is of course important for adolescents as they enter a period of identity management, but also for adults who draw on technologies for social support and connectedness. Our increasingly mobile lifestyle may also mean that technologies are important relationship brokers even within families, and therefore the nuanced ways that we as individuals engage with technology to both manage our own identities and engage with others will be of ever-increasing focus.

The second major theme highlighted in the collection that builds upon the first is dispelling the assumption that online always equates to negative interactions and experiences. While some of the chapters have highlighted the more antisocial aspects associated with online interactions and the need to address these and develop skills for individuals to manage relationships online, other more positive engagements have also been highlighted in the chapters. Such connections online may enable support to protect health and wellbeing and enable a reconfiguration of what 'typical' work may look like through technological facilitation. What we can expect is that technology will become increasingly significant and will impact more areas of our lives in years to come and engaging this for positive benefit should be a focus for future research.

The final theme to be highlighted here reflects the influence of technology across the lifespan, and indeed beyond. Gone are the days when technology was solely viewed through a lens of the young, and the recent global pandemic has highlighted how central technology is to each and every one of us. Individuals are required to 'check-in' to places via QR codes to enable tracking and tracing of COVID-19, which has created a divide for those populations who possess a smartphone with the appropriate technology to allow for this and those who don't. Such requirements have also focused gaze on populations who may have more difficulty in adapting to technology use, for example, older populations. However, what we need to remain mindful of is that we should steer clear of assumptions and stereotypes about any particular group. While some older populations may find technologies difficult, others have embraced these as a way to not only allow for tracing potential outbreaks but also connecting with others and doing social things differently.

The COVID-19 global pandemic has therefore highlighted the importance of technology in our everyday actions both on an individual level to remain connected with others, at a societal and national level to keep abreast of national changes, advice, and restrictions, and also on a global level in reporting and understanding the differential patterns of impact across the world. The expectation that we will 'check-in' via QR codes where we visit and the broader discussions of vaccine passports highlight that technology and our interactions with it will require an increased focus moving forward. We know that there is a lack of research which focuses on technological engagements with individuals who live in the Global South and the possibilities that this affords for not only connection but supporting education, work, and a global community. While we understand that technology impacts individuals across the lifespan we need to more carefully unpack the implications for particular populations such as marginalised groups. Above all, we need to understand how technology can enable us to think differently about possibilities for connection, support, and the crafting of positive identities, drawing on innovative and dynamic research approaches.

INDEX

A
active narrators, 126
age cohort, 32, 34, 38
algorithmic environment, 117
ambient awareness, 63
antisocial, 133
antisocial behaviour, v, 4, 28, 32
  cyberbullying and trolling, vi
antisocial social media behaviour, 34
authenticity, 55
authentic sense of self, 45

B
barriers to technology use
  accessibility, 72, 109, 110
bereavement guidance, 118
bereavement research, 116
biopsychosocial model, 89

C
closure, 126
Communicative affordance
  portability, 3, 63
Covid-19, 82
co-viewing, 20
cultures of mourning, 118
cyberbullying, 28
cyberbullying and internet trolling, 27
cyberpsychology, 3
cyberstalking, 28

D
dead grief concept(s), vii, 6, 118, 121, 124, 128
Depression Anxiety Stress Scale, 103
digital material, 119, 123
digital media use
  adolescence, 45
  daily life, 12, 18
  guidelines for children, 11, 15, 21
  healthy childhood development, 11
  impact on sleep, 19
  mid life responsibilities, 68
  parent influence, 11, 12, 15, 18, 20

sedentary behaviour, 11
sibling influence, 12
toddlers, 64
young adults, 44
young children, v, 4, 9, 15
digital native, 56
digital remains, 124
digital technologies, 44
disability activism, 90
disability research, 89

E
educational programs and apps, 17
emerging adults, 29
employment outcomes, 92
enhancing their social status, 35
entertainment, 17, 20
environmental factors, 110
Erikson's psychosocial model, 28, 29
  generativity psychosocial stage, 31

F
Facebook, 37, 98, 125
  community guidelines, 37
  friends, 100
  health outcomes, 108
  memorialised-profile design, 125
  mental health, 107, 110
  minimum age, 4
  participation in health activities, 109
  social support, 100, 104, 108
  time spent using, 101, 109
Facebook Messenger, 3
face-to-face social interaction, 55
family
  family practices, 18, 19, 62
  friction, 68
  technology use, 10
family caregivers, 83
fathers, 21
flexible working arrangements, 86

flexible working hours, 87
Freud, S., 116

G
gaming consoles, 17
geographical
  barriers, 6, 62
  isolated, 132
  location, 100, 101, 106
  metropolitan, 106
  regional, 98, 107
Global South, 134
grief, 115
grief assumptions, 117
grief norms, 118
grief policing, 119
grief researchers, 121
grief scholarship, 121

H
'help or hinder' discourse, 121

I
identity, 132
identity confusion, 29, 50, 53
identity formation, vi, 5, 30, 35, 45, 46, 54
identity integration, 47, 48
India, 82
informal caregivers, 85
insider perspective, 84
intercoder agreement, 14
intergenerational connectedness, vi, 62, 72
  middle-aged parents, 68
Interpersonal Support Evaluation List, 102

L
laptops and computers, 17

lifespan, 132

M
marginalised groups, 134
medical model, 90
methodological approaches, vii
   content analysis, 9, 14
   cross-sectional and quasi experimental, 33
   diary studies, 12–14, 21
   longitudinal, qualitative data, 116
   online questionnaire, 13
   stratified random cluster, 48
middle-aged adults, 29, 31, 36
Mid-Life, 68
modern informational environment, 122

O
older adults
   'grey digital divide', 69
   technology adoption, 70
online communities, 67
outsider researchers, 84

P
parent supervision, 16
passive agents, 127
peer connectedness, 47, 51, 56
peer support, 50
Perceived Stress Scale, 102
perpetrator profiling, 39
Physical Illness Measure, 103
post-industrial dream, 127
privacy versus connection, vi
psychosocial crisis, 36

Q
quality health care, 91

R
relationship maintenance, 2
remote-work arrangements, 6
rural and remote healthcare, 82

S
Satisfaction with Life Scale, 103
screen time, 10, 15, 19
'second loss', 119, 125
self-esteem, 45, 50, 54, 55
self-presentation, 35, 54
   suitability of internet, 46, 49, 51
smartphones, 15, 17, 133
social capital, 109
social communication, 39
social comparison, 30
social convoy, 37
Social Convoy Model, 28, 31, 36
social grief, 124
social media
   definition, 4
social media use
   adolescents, 65
   older adults, 72
   young adults, 66, 67
   young children, 63, 64
social model of disability, 89
social relationships, 36
social support, 63, 66, 71
   older adults, 71
social support, vi, 2, 5, 98, 99
   Facebook, 100, 104, 108
   face to face, 99, 108
   families, vi
   impact on stress, 99
socio-cultural, 87
Stage models, 116
stages of grief, 118
stereotypes, 133

T

tablets, 17
tech companies, 124
technological facilitation, 133
technology
    definition, 10
    keep children occupied, 20
telehealth, vii, 6, 81
telemedicine, 82
telepractice, 82
televisions, 17
traits, 27
treasured artefacts, 120
trolling, 28

U

Uses of Facebook Scale, 33, 38

V

virtual appointments, 88
VR reunion, 124

W

wellbeing, vi
work-care balance, vii
'work-life collision', 91
workplace-based telehealth, 88
workplace flexibility, 85

Y

young children
    frequency of digital media sessions, 16
    parental supervision, 18
younger adults, 31

GPSR Compliance

The European Union's (EU) General Product Safety Regulation (GPSR) is a set of rules that requires consumer products to be safe and our obligations to ensure this.

If you have any concerns about our products, you can contact us on

ProductSafety@springernature.com

In case Publisher is established outside the EU, the EU authorized representative is:

Springer Nature Customer Service Center GmbH
Europaplatz 3
69115 Heidelberg, Germany

www.ingramcontent.com/pod-product-compliance
Ingram Content Group UK Ltd.
Pitfield, Milton Keynes, MK11 3LW, UK
UKHW021251180426
11946UKWH00004B/83